Simple Home Cooking

Halogen
Recipes

D0907454

Publisher's Note: Raw or semi-cooked eggs should not be consumed by babies, toddlers, pregnant or breastfeeding women, the elderly or those suffering from a chronic illness.

Publisher & Creative Director: Nick Wells
Project Editor: Laura Bulbeck
Art Director: Mike Spender
Layout Design: Jane Ashley
Proofreader: Dawn Laker

Special thanks to Esme Chapman, Emma Chafer and Catherine Taylor

This is a **FLAME TREE** Book

FLAME TREE PUBLISHING
Crabtree Hall, Crabtree Lane
Fulham, London SW6 6TY
United Kingdom
www.flametreepublishing.com

First published 2013

13 15 17 16 14
3 5 7 9 10 8 6 4 2

ISBN: 978-0-85775-812-5

A copy of the CIP data for this book is available from the British Library.

Thanks to JML (www.JMLdirect.com) for providing the images on pages 11, 12, 15 and to shef for the images on pages 9 and 10.

All other images courtesy of Flame Tree Publishing Ltd except for the following, which are courtesy of Shutterstock and © the following contributors: 13 Christopher Elwell; 14 Joshua Resnick; 16 ElenaGaak; 19t fourth of four; 19b Robyn Mackenzie; 21 Gayvoronskaya_Yana; 23 Martin Turzak.

Printed in Singapore

Simple Home Cooking

Halogen Recipes

**FLAME TREE
PUBLISHING**

Contents

č

Equipment & Techniques

With their impressive credentials for producing healthier and tastier meals, halogen ovens have never been more popular. Beginning with a practical introduction to your halogen oven, this chapter will bring you up to speed on the techniques needed to uncover the secrets of successful roasting, grilling and baking. In no time at all, you'll be impressing your friends and family with your effortless command of this revolutionary cooking method.

Introducing Halogen Ovens

Halogen cooking is a new and innovative way of cooking which is rapidly rising in popularity and has been recognised as one of the best pieces of equipment for today's busy lifestyle. You will discover, when you begin cooking in the stylish, modern and intriguing machine that is a halogen oven, how easy it is to use. It can save you time, energy and, even better, money.

What is a Halogen Oven?

A halogen oven is a portable, freestanding tabletop oven. It is powered by a halogen element (bulb), which produces infrared rays, and these combine with powerful electricity currents circulating hot air around the food to be cooked. The intense heat cooks food quickly without the necessity of turning the food round or over, as the hot air circulates around the food. As the heat is almost instant, there is no need to preheat the oven. This also means that the heat switches off almost instantaneously.

- The Oven – The halogen oven consists of a large glass bowl in which the food to be cooked is placed, generally on one of the two racks which are supplied. The bowl sits in a rigid, normally plastic base stand. It is important that the two steel racks, the high rack and the low rack, are used in the oven so that the hot air is free to circulate around the food. There is also an extender ring, which sits in the base to make the oven larger, plus a pair of tongs to use with the oven.

- The Lid – The halogen element is located in the lid. The lid handle must be used to lift the lid on and off the oven. The handle also acts as a safety device – when switching the oven on the handle must be pushed down flat in order for you to start cooking. As soon as it is lifted up the oven will switch off. The lid should be carefully placed in the lid stand after the cooking has finished. It is best to leave the lid in the stand to cool before moving it to wipe clean.

- Switches – Also on the lid are two control switches: one is the temperature gauge, which ranges from 120–250°C//250–500°F and the other is the timer, which will run from 0–60 minutes. The timer switch must be turned clockwise only; it should not be turned anti-clockwise, as this may result in damaging the halogen oven. Once the temperature is reached, the light will go off. The light will fluctuate on and off in order to keep the oven at the correct temperature. The timer switch will continue to tick down to zero. You will notice a slight noise from the oven; this is the motor running and the hot air circulation around the food.

Choosing Your Oven

It is important to work out what you want from your halogen oven before buying, to make sure it fits your requirements. Look at the price and what you are getting for your money – most ovens come with the basics: two racks and a pair of tongs, plus most have an extender, which makes the oven larger. When choosing a halogen oven, there are a few points to consider.

First, are you going to use the oven on a regular basis? If so, how many people do you cook for? If it is at least four people, buy a larger oven, one with an extension ring. Remember, when cooking for larger numbers you can always use your conventional oven or microwave to cook the vegetables and the halogen oven for the main dish.

Equipment & Techniques   10

To use, remember it is portable, so it is ideal to take on self-catering holidays. Ensure that wherever you use the oven it is not under wall kitchen cupboards that may catch fire and that it is sitting on a flameproof surface. Also the flex from the oven to the plug is not very long and you need to have space around the oven. You also need to leave 5cm/2 inches between the top of the food and the lid.

Why Use a Halogen Oven?

The halogen oven is efficient, saving both time and money; is portable; will happily stand on a work surface; is easy to use; is versatile, as any cooking methods can be used; and provides succulent, moist roasts as well as delicious desserts, cakes and bakes.

- **Multi-purpose** – First, remember that the halogen oven will cook all the foods that your conventional oven will. It bakes, roasts, grills, steams and fries; as well as defrosting and reheating. Food can also be dried, such as sun-dried tomatoes, and blanched, such as fresh vegetables to be frozen and sterilized. Some foods, especially fish, can be seasoned when first bought and then frozen. When wishing to use, there is no need to defrost first. Place the fish in the oven and defrost, then switch the oven to bake and cook.

- **Efficiency** – The hot air that circulates the food during cooking will ensure that the food is evenly browned thanks to the even cooking the halogen oven gives. In some instances, you will discover that the conventional cooking time is reduced, giving a more efficient method of cooking, which saves you money as well as time. The other reason it's more efficient is that it uses half the electricity that the microwave oven and conventional oven use.

∾ **Ease of Use** – Most halogen ovens have a self-cleaning programme. Set the programme and, when finished, simply wipe the bowl clean. Also, the clear bowl enables you to watch the food whilst it is cooking, so you can see if it is ready before the time.

The second advantage is that with a conventional oven, the door is opened repeatedly to check the food. This can make the cook hot and bothered. This does not happen with the halogen oven.

∾ **The Food** – Food needs little or no oil or fat, even when frying. If you wish, you can cook your roasts straight on the rack, thus removing much of the fat. So if you wish to be healthier or are concerned about your diet, the halogen oven is an excellent solution. Further good points are the improved taste and, in some cases, texture of the food. What's great is that the food does not dry out, so it is more moist and succulent with a fresher taste.

Equipment

∾ Most halogen ovens come with a lid rack, but if not supplied, then it is a good idea to get one. This will mean that once cooking has finished and the timer switch has ticked down to zero, the lid can carefully be removed and placed in the rack and left until cool.

∾ One of the most important items is a pair of very sturdy oven gloves or gauntlet gloves for handling the cooked dishes.

- Check that your ovenware (and lids, if applicable) fit in the oven with room for the hot air to circulate. Ovenproof bowls, ovenproof plates, cake tins and small trays are a good investment, as many of your conventional baking trays or sheets may not fit.

- If using your own crockery, ensure it is ovenproof. Under no circumstances should you be tempted to use delicate plates or dishes, as they will surely crack or break.

- Kitchen foil can be used and is ideal for covering dishes such as casseroles. It can also be used to make parcels for steaming when cooking fish or vegetables. Kitchen foil can be used to line the rack in order to prevent food dropping through the rack. Baking parchment can also be used, but avoid using other papers in the oven.

Cleaning Your Oven

Most halogen ovens have a self-cleaning programme. If this applies to your oven, simply follow the manufacturer's instructions.

To clean manually, allow the oven to cool, then remove any bits of food and drain off juices or fat if necessary. Pour in about 10 cm/4 inches of warm water with a little mild washing up liquid if very dirty, otherwise just use clean water. Replace the lid and lock. Switch the oven to the correct wash programme and turn the timer to the correct time, usually 10–15 minutes. When finished, unlock and cool before discarding the water and wipe the glass bowl with a clean cloth. If washing up liquid was used, rinse in clean water before drying. Never immerse the lid into water – simply wipe clean with a damp cloth. If liked, the bowl and racks can be washed in a dishwasher.

Cooking in Your Halogen Oven

❦

Before starting to cook, carefully read the manufacturer's instruction guidelines. Keep the booklet handy until you are entirely confident on how to use the halogen oven and very soon you will be serving both family and friends delicious dishes any chef would be proud to present.

First Steps

Once all the equipment has been sorted, you are ready to start cooking. It is important that a few guidelines are followed in order not to have any mishaps. You may find that it will take a little time to get used to this method of cooking and a little tweaking and experimenting is necessary when cooking, especially with cakes and bakes.

Making Toast – First, try with something simple such as a piece of toast. Ensure that there is space around the halogen oven so that the hot lid can easily be removed once the toast is ready, and that there is at least 5 cm/2 inches between the food and the halogen element.

Place the glass bowl in the base stand, then place the high rack in the glass bowl. Arrange 1–2 slices of bread on the rack. Plug the power socket into the power point. Place the lid in position, making sure that the handle is upright. Once the lid is in place, push the handle down to lock. Remember to ensure that there is a 5 cm/2 inch gap between the lid and the top of the food, otherwise the food may burn.

Turn the timer switch clockwise to the selected time, in this case 3–5 minutes. A light will then come on. The oven will switch off when the set temperature is reached. If the light comes on again, it is because the temperature dipped and will switch off when the correct temperature is reached again. A bell or a buzzer will sound when the time is up. Remove the lid carefully and place in the stand. Using the oven tongs remove the toast, then enjoy!

∾ Taking It Further – You can now see how easy it is, so it's time to cook something else. Why not try a more complicated recipe, such as Roast Chicken (*see* page 140). Remember, there is no need to preheat the halogen oven before placing the chicken inside.

Cooking Methods

The halogen oven will bake, fry, roast, grill, steam and defrost. Below are a few tips on how to achieve perfect results.

∾ Roasting – Fix the extender and place the low rack in the glass bowl. If a joint or whole chicken, calculate the cooking time (*see* page 17). Wrap in kitchen foil if preferred. Place in a roasting tin small enough so that the hot air can freely circulate. Place the lid in position and push the handle down.

For a chicken, set the halogen oven to 200°C/400°F and cook for 50 minutes, then reduce the heat to 190°C/375°F and remove the kitchen foil if used. Continue to cook for 20–30 minutes until cooked. Remove from the oven and allow to rest for 5–10 minutes before carving.

For a leg of lamb, prepare as above, wrapping in kitchen foil and cooking at 200°C/400°F for 40 minutes. Reduce the temperature to 190°C/375°F, open up the kitchen foil and cook for a further 20–30 minutes. Allow to rest for at least 10 minutes before carving.

∾ Frying – Set the halogen oven to 200°C/400°F. Place the food to be fried on the high rack and place in the oven. Replace the lid and secure. Cook for 6–8 minutes, remove the lid and serve.

∾ Grilling – Set the halogen oven to 200°C/400°F. Place on the high rack and put into the hot oven. Close the lid and cook for 5–10 minutes, or according to the recipe. Remove lid and serve.

∾ Steaming – Set the halogen oven to 200°C/400°F. If steaming vegetables, either place in a heatproof container with a lid or wrap in kitchen foil. Add 2–3 tablespoons of water or stock, wrap tightly and place on the low rack in the oven. Secure the lid and steam. Broccoli or sprouts need 15–20 minutes. Potatoes, carrots and other root vegetables require longer, at least 40–50 minutes. Reduce the time for fish by about 10 minutes.

∾ Baking – Set the halogen oven to 180°C/350°F and prepare the cake tin, making sure that it will fit in the oven. Make the cake mixture, spoon into the tin and level the top. Place the low rack and extender into the oven and put the cake tin on top. Close the lid and cook according to the recipe. If using your own recipe, you may find the timing and temperature need checking, so you should watch carefully.

You will soon get to know what temperature and timings produce the best results. Remove the cooked cake and leave until cool before removing from the tin.

∞ Defrosting – Fit the extender to the halogen oven and use either rack, depending on how much you are defrosting. Remember that the top of the food must be 5 cm/2 inches below the lid. Put the food on the rack and add the lid, keeping the handle raised. Turn the temperature switch to 'thaw' and set the timer. Place the handle down. The red and green lights will come on, as well as the halogen bulb under the lid. The red light will go on and off as the low temperature is retained. Turn the food occasionally and when the time is up, check it is thoroughly defrosted. If it is not, return to the oven for a little longer.

Temperatures and Timings

The cooking times given here can only be approximate, as the time will vary according to the shape and size of the food. For example, a thick piece of steak will take longer than a long, thin piece. The more you cook in the halogen oven, the more adept you will become in gauging the correct cooking temperature and time, and then you will be able to use your own recipes confidently.

∞ Roast Beef (1 kg/2 lb 3 oz piece) cook at 190°C/375°F–200°C/400°F for 1–1¼ hours on the low rack.

∞ Steak (175 g/6 oz piece) cook at 200°C/400°F for 12–15 minutes for medium or 14–18 minutes for well done, all on the high rack.

∞ Whole chicken (1.3 kg/3 lb) cook at 190°C/375°F for 1¼–1½ hours on the low rack.

∞ Boneless chicken (175 g/6 oz portion) cook at 190°C/375°F for 15–20 minutes on the high rack.

- Sausages cook at 200°C/400°F for 12–15 minutes on the high rack

- Bacon rashers (single layer) cook at 200°C/400°F for 8–12 minutes, depending how crispy you want, on the high rack.

- Fish fillet (175 g/6 oz piece, wrapped) cook at 200°C/400°F for 12 minutes on the high rack.

- Onion (1 medium) cut into quarters and roast at 200°C/400°F for 45–55 minutes, or finely chop and cook for 30–35 minutes. Cook either on the high or low rack.

- Chopped carrots cook at 200°C/400°F for 45–55 minutes on the high or low rack.

- Assorted vegetables (such as beans, sliced peppers, fresh peas, courgette or broccoli) cook at 200°C/400°F for 15–25 minutes on the high or low rack.

- Baked potato (175 g/6 oz) cook at 200°C/400°F for 45–50 minutes on the high or low rack.

- New potatoes cook at 200°C/400°F for 40–55 minutes on the high or low rack.

Important Points to Remember

- Keep the cookbook and manufacturer's manual nearby for quick reference.

- There is no need to preheat the halogen oven.

- Calculate the cooking time and temperature first. Remember that vegetables will take longer than meat or fish, so when calculating, the vegetables will often go in first.

- Ensure that the dish or tin will fit comfortably in the oven with plenty of space for the hot air to circulate.

- Do not leave the oven plugged into the socket when not in use.

- Stand the oven on a heatproof work surface with plenty of room around and not under a cupboard, which could catch fire.

- Ensure there is room to place the lid in the stand to cool down when the cooking is finished and use sturdy oven gloves to handle the hot parts after cooking.

- Do not leave the oven unattended when in use and check the food occasionally. You may find with some foods that they need turning, especially those near the glass.

- If food appears to be cooking too fast, cover with kitchen foil.

- Do not turn the timer switch backwards once the food is cooked.

- Remove food from the oven once cooked, otherwise bacteria may build up in the glass bowl.

- Leave a 5 cm/2 inch gap between the lid and the top of the food.

- The most important factor when using the oven is to ensure that all of the oven, including the flex, is out of reach of small children and pets.

With all that in mind, have fun experimenting and good luck.

Hygiene in the Kitchen

૮

It is well worth remembering that many foods can carry some form of bacteria. In most cases, the worst it will lead to is a bout of food poisoning or gastroenteritis, although for certain people this can be more serious. The risk can be reduced or eliminated by good food hygiene and proper cooking.

Do not buy food that is past its sell-by date and do not consume any food that is past its use-by date. When buying food, use your eyes and nose. If the food looks tired, limp or a bad colour or it has a rank, acrid or simply bad smell, do not buy or eat it under any circumstances. Do take special care when preparing raw meat and fish.

A separate chopping board should be used for each food; wash the knife, board and the hands thoroughly before handling or preparing any other food.

Regularly clean, defrost and clear out the refrigerator or freezer – it is worth checking the packaging to see exactly how long each product is safe to freeze.

Avoid handling food if suffering from an upset stomach, as bacteria can be passed on through food preparation.

Dish cloths and tea towels must be washed and changed regularly. Ideally, use disposable cloths, which should be replaced on a daily basis. More durable cloths should be left to soak in bleach, then washed in the washing machine on a boil wash.

Keep hands, cooking utensils and food preparation surfaces clean and do not allow pets to climb onto any work surfaces.

Buying

Avoid bulk buying where possible, especially fresh produce such as meat, poultry, fish, fruit and vegetables, unless buying for the freezer. Fresh foods lose their nutritional value rapidly, so buying a little at a time minimises loss of nutrients. It also eliminates a packed refrigerator, which reduces the effectiveness of the refrigeration process.

When buying prepackaged goods such as cans or pots of cream and yogurts, check that the packaging is intact and not damaged or pierced at all. Cans should not be dented, pierced or rusty. Check the sell-by dates even for cans and packets of dry ingredients such as flour and rice. Store fresh foods in the refrigerator as soon as possible – not in the car or the office.

When buying frozen foods, ensure that they are not heavily iced on the outside and the contents feel completely frozen. Ensure that the frozen foods have been stored in the cabinet at the correct storage level and the temperature is below -18˚C/-0.4˚F. Pack in cool bags to transport home and place in the freezer as soon as possible after purchase.

Preparation

Make sure that all work surfaces and utensils are clean and dry. Hygiene should be given priority at all times. Separate chopping boards should be used for raw and cooked meats, fish and vegetables. Currently, a variety of good-quality plastic boards come in various designs and colours. This makes differentiating easier and the plastic has the added hygienic

Hygiene in the Kitchen

advantage of being washable at high temperatures in the dishwasher. (NB: If using the board for fish, first wash in cold water, then in hot, to prevent odour!) Also, remember that knives and utensils should always be thoroughly cleaned after use.

When cooking, be particularly careful to keep cooked and raw food separate to avoid any contamination. It is worth washing all fruits and vegetables, regardless of whether they are going to be eaten raw or lightly cooked. This rule should apply even to prewashed herbs and salads.

Do not reheat food more than once. If using a microwave, always check that the food is piping hot all the way through. In theory, the food should reach a minimum temperature of 70°C/158°F and needs to be cooked at that temperature for at least 3 minutes to ensure that any bacteria in the food are killed.

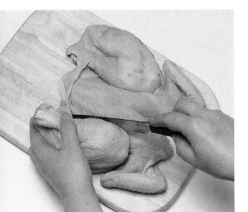

All poultry must be thoroughly thawed before using, including chicken and poussin. Remove the food to be thawed from the freezer and place in a shallow dish to contain the juices.

Leave the food in the refrigerator until it is completely thawed. A 1.4 kg/3 lb whole chicken will take about 26–30 hours to thaw. To speed up the process, immerse the chicken in cold water. However, make sure that the water is changed regularly. When the joints can move freely and no ice crystals remain in the cavity, the bird is completely thawed.

Once thawed, remove the wrapper and pat the chicken dry. Place the chicken in a shallow dish, cover lightly and if storing, store as close to the base of the refrigerator as possible. The chicken should be cooked as soon as possible.

Some foods can be cooked from frozen, including many prepacked foods such as soups, sauces, casseroles and breads. Where applicable, follow the manufacturers' instructions.

Vegetables and fruits can also be cooked from frozen, but meats and fish should be thawed first. The only time food can be refrozen is when the food has been thoroughly thawed, then cooked. Once the food has cooled, then it can be frozen again. On such occasions, the food can only be stored for one month.

All poultry and game (except for duck) must be cooked thoroughly. When cooked, the juices will run clear from the thickest part of the bird – the best area to try is usually the thigh. Other meats, such as minced meat and pork, should be cooked right the way through. Fish should turn opaque, be firm in texture and break easily into large flakes.

When cooking leftovers, make sure they are reheated until piping hot and that any sauce or soup reaches boiling point first before eating.

Storing, Refrigerating and Freezing

Meat, poultry, fish, seafood and dairy products should all be refrigerated. The temperature of the refrigerator should be between 1–5°C/34–41°F, while the freezer temperature should not rise above -18°C/-0.4°F.

To ensure the optimum refrigerator and freezer temperature, avoid leaving the door open for a long time. Try not to overstock the refrigerator, as this reduces the airflow inside and affects the

efficiency in cooling the food within. When refrigerating cooked food, allow it to cool down quickly and completely before refrigerating. Hot food will raise the temperature of the refrigerator and possibly affect or spoil other food stored in it.

Food within the refrigerator and freezer should always be covered. Raw and cooked food should be stored in separate parts of the refrigerator. Cooked food should be kept on the top shelves of the refrigerator, while raw meat, poultry and fish should be placed on bottom shelves to avoid drips and cross-contamination.

It is recommended that eggs should be refrigerated in order to maintain their freshness and shelf life.

Take care that frozen foods are not stored in the freezer for too long. Blanched vegetables can be stored for one month; beef, lamb, poultry and pork for six months; and unblanched vegetables and fruits in syrup for a year. Oily fish and sausages can be stored for three months. Dairy products can last four to six months, while cakes and pastries can be kept in the freezer for three to six months.

High-risk Foods

Certain foods may carry risks to people who are considered vulnerable, such as the elderly, the ill, pregnant or breastfeeding women, babies, young infants and those suffering from a recurring illness. It is advisable to avoid those foods listed below, which belong to a higher-risk category.

There is a slight chance that some eggs carry the bacteria salmonella. Cook eggs until both the yolk and the white are firm to eliminate this risk.

Pay particular attention to dishes and products incorporating lightly cooked or raw eggs, which should be eliminated from the diet. Sauces including Hollandaise, mayonnaise, mousses, soufflés and meringues all use raw or lightly cooked eggs, as do custard-based dishes, ice creams and sorbets. These are all considered high-risk foods to the vulnerable groups mentioned above.

Certain meats and poultry also carry the potential risk of salmonella and so should be cooked thoroughly until the juices run clear and there is no pinkness left. Unpasteurised products such as milk, cheese (especially soft cheese), pâté and meat (both raw and cooked) all have the potential risk of listeria and should be avoided.

When buying seafood, buy from a reputable source which has a high turnover to ensure freshness. Fish should have bright, clear eyes, shiny skin and bright pink or red gills. The fish should feel stiff to the touch, with a slight smell of sea air and iodine. The flesh of fish steaks and fillets should be translucent, with no signs of discolouration.

Molluscs such as scallops, clams and mussels are sold fresh and are still alive. Avoid any that are open or do not close when tapped lightly. In the same way, univalves such as whelks or winkles should withdraw back into their shells when lightly prodded. When choosing cephalopods such as squid and octopus, they should have a firm flesh and pleasant sea smell.

As with all fish, whether it is shellfish or wet fish, care is required when freezing it. It is imperative to check whether the fish has been frozen before. If it has been frozen, then it should not be frozen again under any circumstances.

Hygiene in the Kitchen

Starters
& Snacks

Whether you are looking for a light lunch, a fancy opening dish for a dinner party or simply a tasty and nutritious snack, this chapter has a great array of recipes on offer. From impressive Garlic Wild Mushroom Galettes to such comforting classics as Cheese-encrusted Potato Scones and Smoked Salmon Quiche, these dishes are a delicious way to perfect your halogen cooking techniques before moving on to the main meals.

Potato Skins

Serves 4

4 large baking potatoes
2 tbsp olive oil
2 tsp paprika
125 g/4 oz pancetta, roughly chopped
6 tbsp double cream
125 g/4 oz Gorgonzola cheese
1 tbsp freshly chopped parsley

To serve:

mayonnaise
sweet chilli dipping sauce
tossed green salad

Place the low rack in the halogen oven and set the oven to 200˚C/400˚F. Scrub the potatoes, then prick a few times with a fork or skewer and, when the temperature is reached, place the potatoes directly on the low rack. Close the lid and bake in the oven for 50–60 minutes until tender. The potatoes are cooked when they yield gently to the pressure of your hand.

Remove from the oven and leave the potatoes until cool enough to handle. Cut in half and scoop the flesh into a bowl. Line the low rack with kitchen foil and place in the bowl. Mix together the oil and the paprika and use half to brush the outside of the potato skins and place on the rack. Close the oven lid and cook at 200˚C/400˚F for 5 minutes, or until crisp. Open the oven and remove the potato skins.

Pour the remaining paprika-flavoured oil into a small bowl and stir in the pancetta. Place in the oven and close the lid. Cook for 5 minutes, or until crisp. Open the oven and remove the pancetta. Stir the pancetta into the potato flesh along with the cream, Gorgonzola cheese and parsley. Halve the potato skins and fill with the Gorgonzola filling. Return to the oven, close the lid and cook for a further 10–15 minutes to heat through. Sprinkle with a little more paprika and serve immediately with mayonnaise, sweet chilli sauce and a green salad.

Hot Tiger Prawns with Parma Ham

Serves 4

1/2 cucumber, peeled if preferred
4 ripe tomatoes
12 raw tiger prawns
6 tbsp olive oil
4 garlic cloves, peeled and crushed
4 tbsp freshly chopped parsley
salt and freshly ground black pepper
6 slices Parma ham, cut in half
4 slices Italian flat bread
4 tbsp dry white wine

Peel the cucumber and tomatoes thinly, then arrange on four large plates and reserve. Peel the prawns, leaving the tail shell intact and remove the thin black vein running down the back.

Whisk together 4 tablespoons of the olive oil, the garlic and chopped parsley in a small bowl and season with plenty of salt and pepper. Add the prawns to the mixture and stir until they are well coated. Remove the prawns, then wrap each one in a piece of Parma ham and secure with a cocktail stick.

Place the low rack in the halogen oven and set the oven to 190°C/375°F. Place the prepared prawns in a lightly oiled dish with the bread slices and cook in the oven for 5 minutes.

Remove the prawns from the oven and spoon the wine over the prawns and bread. Return to the oven and cook for a further 10 minutes until piping hot.

Carefully remove the cocktail sticks and arrange 3 prawn rolls on each slice of bread. Place on top of the sliced cucumber and tomatoes and serve immediately.

Smoked Salmon Quiche

Serves 6

225 g/8 oz plain flour
50 g/2 oz butter
50 g/2 oz white vegetable fat or lard
2 tsp sunflower oil
225 g/8 oz potato, peeled and diced
125 g/4 oz Gruyère cheese, grated
75 g/3 oz smoked salmon trimmings
4 medium eggs, beaten
250 ml/8 fl oz single cream
salt and freshly ground black pepper
1 tbsp freshly chopped
flat-leaf parsley

To serve:

mixed salad
baby new potatoes

Fit the extender to the halogen oven bowl and place the low rack in the oven. Set the oven to 190°C/375°F. Blend the flour, butter and white vegetable fat or lard together until it resembles fine breadcrumbs. Blend again, adding sufficient water to make a firm but pliable dough. Use the dough to line a 20.5 cm/8 inch flan dish or tin, then chill the pastry case in the refrigerator for 30 minutes. Bake blind for 12–15 minutes.

Pour the oil into a small, heatproof bowl, add the diced potato and cook in the oven for 5 minutes, or until lightly browned and tender. Remove from the oven and leave to cool.

Scatter the grated cheese evenly over the base of the pastry case, then arrange the cooled potato on top. Add the smoked salmon in an even layer.

Beat the eggs with the cream and season with salt and pepper. Whisk in the parsley and pour the mixture carefully into the pastry case.

Reduce the oven temperature to 180°C/350°F and bake for about 20–25 minutes, or until the filling is set and golden. Cover with kitchen foil if browning too quickly. Serve hot or cold with a mixed salad and baby new potatoes.

Oven-baked Pork Balls with Peppers

Serves 4

For the garlic bread:

2–4 garlic cloves, peeled
50 g/2 oz butter, softened
1 tbsp freshly chopped parsley
2–3 tsp lemon juice
1 focaccia loaf

For the pork balls:

350 g/12 oz fresh pork mince
4 tbsp freshly chopped basil
2 garlic cloves, peeled and chopped
3 sun-dried tomatoes, chopped
salt and freshly ground black pepper
3 tbsp olive oil
1 small red pepper, deseeded and
cut into chunks
1 small green pepper, deseeded
and cut into chunks
1 small yellow pepper, deseeded
and cut into chunks
175 g/6 oz cherry tomatoes

Place the low rack in the halogen oven and set the oven to 190°C/375°F. Crush the garlic, then blend with the softened butter, the parsley and enough lemon juice to give a soft consistency. Shape into a roll, wrap in baking parchment and chill in the refrigerator for at least 30 minutes.

Mix together the pork, basil, 1 chopped garlic clove, sun-dried tomatoes and seasoning until well combined. With damp hands, divide the mixture into 12–16 pieces, roll into balls and reserve.

Pour the olive oil into the dish. Place in the oven and heat for 3–5 minutes until very hot. Remove from the oven and add the pork balls, the remaining chopped garlic and the peppers. Return to the oven and cook for 15 minutes. Remove from the oven and stir in the cherry tomatoes and season with salt and pepper. Return to the oven and continue to cook for a further 10 minutes. Remove from the oven and leave to stand while toasting the bread. Switch the low rack for the high rack.

Slice the bread, place on the high rack and close the lid. Cook at 200°C/400°F for 3–5 minutes until lightly toasted, then spread with the prepared garlic butter. Stir the vinegar into the pork balls and serve with the garlic bread.

Stuffed Onions with Pine Nuts

Serves 4

4 medium onions, peeled
2 garlic cloves, peeled and crushed
2 tbsp fresh brown breadcrumbs
4 tbsp white breadcrumbs
25 g/1 oz sultanas
25 g/1 oz pine nuts
50 g/2 oz low-fat hard cheese such as Edam, grated
2 tbsp freshly chopped parsley
salt and freshly ground black pepper
1 medium egg, beaten
salad leaves, to serve

Place the low rack in the halogen oven and set the oven to 200˚C/400˚F. Place the onions in a dish and pour in 150 ml/¼ pint water. Cover lightly with kitchen foil and place in the oven. Cook for 15 minutes, then test to see if the onions are tender. If not, continue to cook for a further 5 minutes.

Drain well. Allow the onions to cool, then slice each one in half horizontally. Scoop out most of the onion flesh, but leave a reasonably firm shell.

Chop 4 tablespoons of the onion flesh and place in a bowl with the crushed garlic, brown breadcrumbs, 2 tbsp of the white breadcrumbs, the sultanas, pine nuts, grated cheese and parsley. Season with salt and pepper. Stir well and bind together with as much of the beaten egg as necessary to make a firm filling.

Pile the mixture back into the onion shells and top with the remaining breadcrumbs. Place in an oiled ovenproof dish and return to the oven. Switch the timer to 20 minutes and close the lid. Cook for the hole 20 minutes, or until golden brown. Serve immediately with the salad leaves.

Rosemary Olive Focaccia

Makes 2 loaves

700 g/1^1/$_2$ lb strong white flour
pinch salt
pinch caster sugar
7 g/^{1}/$_4$ oz sachet easy-blend
dried yeast
2 tsp freshly chopped rosemary
450 ml/^{3}/$_4$ pint warm water
3 tbsp olive oil
75 g/3 oz pitted black olives,
roughly chopped
rosemary sprigs, to garnish

To finish:

3 tbsp olive oil
coarse sea salt
freshly ground black pepper

Fit the extender to the halogen oven bowl and put the low rack in the oven. Set the oven to 200°C/400°F. Sift the flour, salt and sugar into a large bowl. Stir in the yeast and rosemary. Make a well in the centre.

Pour in the warm water and the oil and mix to a soft dough. Turn out onto a lightly floured surface and knead for about 10 minutes until smooth and elastic. Pat the olives dry on kitchen paper, then gently knead into the dough. Put in an oiled bowl, cover with clingfilm and leave to rise in a warm place for 1^1/$_2$ hours, or until it has doubled in size.

Turn out the dough and knead again for a minute or two. Divide in half and roll out each piece to a 23 cm/9 inch circle. Transfer to an oiled ovenproof plate that will fit in the oven, cover with oiled clingfilm and leave to rise for 30 minutes. Using the fingertips, make deep dimples all over the dough. Drizzle with the oil and sprinkle with sea salt.

Bake separately in the oven for 20–25 minutes until risen and golden. Cover the top with kitchen foil if browning too quickly. Cool on a wire rack and garnish with sprigs of rosemary. Grind over a little black pepper before serving.

Garlic Wild Mushroom Galettes

Serves 6

For the quick flaky pastry:

125 g/4 oz butter
175 g/6 oz plain flour
pinch of salt

For the filling:

1 onion, peeled
1 red chilli, deseeded
2 garlic cloves, peeled
275 g/10 oz mixed mushrooms
e.g. oyster, chestnut, morels, ceps
and chanterelles
25 g/1 oz butter
2 tbsp freshly chopped parsley
125 g/4 oz mozzarella
cheese, sliced

To serve:

cherry tomatoes
mixed green salad leaves

Place the low rack in the halogen oven and set the oven to 190˚C/375˚F. Place the butter in the freezer for 30 minutes. Sift the flour and salt into a large bowl. Grate the butter using the coarse side of a grater, dipping the butter in the flour every now and again, as it makes it easier to grate. Mix the butter into the flour using a knife, making sure all the butter is coated thoroughly. Add 2 tablespoons cold water and continue to mix, bringing the mixture together. Use your hands to complete the mixing. Add a little more water if needed to leave a clean bowl. Place the pastry in a polythene bag and chill in the refrigerator for 30 minutes.

Roll out the chilled pastry very thinly. Cut out six 15 cm/6 inch circles and place on a lightly oiled baking sheet or small tray. Thinly slice the onion, divide into rings and reserve. Thinly slice the chilli and garlic into wafer-thin slivers. Add to the onion and reserve. Wipe the mushrooms. Halve or quarter any large mushrooms and keep the small ones whole.

Melt the butter in a saucepan. Add the onion, chilli and garlic and cook for 5 minutes. Add the mushrooms and cook in the oven for a further 5 minutes. Remove from the heat. Stir the parsley into the mixture and drain off any excess liquid. Pile the mixture onto the pastry circles within 5 mm/1⁄4 inch of the edge. Arrange the cheese on top. Do this in two batches or make one 23 cm/9 inch pastry round. Bake for 12–15 minutes until golden brown and serve with the tomatoes and salad.

Seafood Parcels

Serves 4

225 g/8 oz pappardelle or tagliatelle
8 raw tiger prawns, shelled
8 raw queen scallops
175 g/6 oz baby squid, cleaned and
cut into rings
4 tbsp dry white wine
4 thin lemon slices

For the pesto:

50 g/2 oz fresh coriander leaves
1 garlic clove, peeled
25 g/1 oz pine nuts, toasted
1 tsp lemon juice
5 tbsp olive oil
1 tbsp grated Parmesan cheese
salt and freshly ground black pepper

Place the low rack in the halogen oven and set the oven to 180°C/350°F.

To make the pesto, blend the coriander leaves, garlic, pine nuts and lemon juice with 1 tablespoon of the olive oil to a smooth paste in a food processor. With the motor running slowly, add the remaining oil. Stir the Parmesan cheese into the pesto and season with salt and pepper.

Bring a pan of lightly salted water to a rolling boil. Add the pasta and cook for 3 minutes only. Drain thoroughly, return to the pan and spoon over two thirds of the pesto. Toss to coat.

Cut out 4 circles, about 30 cm/12 inches in diameter, from nonstick baking parchment. Spoon the pasta onto one half of each circle. Top each pile of pasta with 2 prawns, 3 scallops and a few squid rings. Spoon 1 tablespoon wine over each serving, then drizzle with the remaining coriander pesto and top with a slice of lemon.

Close the parcels by folding over the other half of the paper, to make a semi-circle, then turn and twist the edges of the paper to secure. You may need to do this in two batches, or make 1 large parcel about 23 cm/9 inches in diameter. Place the parcels on a baking tray or round, ovenproof plate. Put on the rack and bake for 15 minutes, or until the fish is cooked. Serve the parcels immediately, allowing each person to open their own.

Bacon, Mushroom Cheese Puffs

Serves 4

1 tbsp olive oil
225 g/8 oz field mushrooms, wiped
and roughly chopped
225 g/8 oz rindless streaky bacon,
roughly chopped
2 tbsp freshly chopped parsley
salt and freshly ground
black pepper
350 g/12 oz ready-rolled puff pastry
sheets, thawed if frozen
25 g/1 oz Emmenthal
cheese, grated
1 medium egg, beaten
salad leaves, such as rocket or
watercress, to garnish
tomatoes, to serve

Fit the extender to the halogen oven bowl and put the low rack inside. Set the oven to 190°C/375°F. Heat the olive oil in a medium saucepan and add the mushrooms and bacon. Fry for 6–8 minutes until golden in colour. Remove and stir in the parsley, season with salt and pepper, then cool.

Roll the sheet of pastry a little thinner on a lightly floured surface to a 30.5 cm/12 inch square. Cut the pastry into 4 equal squares.

Stir the grated Emmenthal cheese into the mushroom mixture. Spoon a quarter of the mixture on to one half of each square.

Brush the edges of the square with a little of the beaten egg. Fold over the pastry to form a triangular parcel. Seal the edges well and place on a small, lightly oiled tray or ovenproof plate. Repeat until the squares are finished.

Make shallow slashes in the top of the pastry with a knife. Brush the parcels with the remaining beaten egg. Place on the rack and cook in the oven for 18–20 minutes until puffy and golden brown. Serve warm or cold, garnished with the salad leaves and served with tomatoes.

Fennel Caramelised Shallot Tartlets

Serves 6

For the cheese pastry:

176 g/6 oz plain white flour
75 g/3 oz slightly salted butter
50 g/2 oz Gruyère cheese, grated
1 small egg yolk

For the filling:

2 tbsp olive oil
225 g/8 oz shallots, peeled
and halved
1 fennel bulb, trimmed and sliced
1 tsp soft brown sugar
1 medium egg
150 ml/$^1/_4$ pint double cream
salt and freshly ground black pepper
25 g/1 oz Gruyère cheese, grated
$^1/_2$ tsp ground cinnamon
mixed salad leaves, to serve

Place the low rack in the halogen oven and set the oven to 190°C/375°F. Sift the flour into a bowl, then rub in the butter, using the fingertips. Stir in the cheese, then add the egg yolk with about 2 tablespoons cold water. Mix to a firm dough, then knead lightly. Wrap in clingfilm and chill in the refrigerator for 30 minutes.

Roll out the pastry on a lightly floured surface and use to line six 10 cm/ 4 inch individual flan or patty tins, about 2 cm/$^3/_4$ inch deep.

Line the pastry cases with baking paper and fill with baking beans or rice. Bake blind in the oven for 10 minutes, remove from the oven and discard paper and beans.

Heat the oil into a saucepan, add the shallots and fennel and cook, stirring occasionally for 5 minutes. Sprinkle the shallots with the sugar, then cook for a further 10 minutes. Remove, stir and cool.

Beat together the egg and cream and season with salt and pepper. Divide the shallot mixture between the pastry cases. Pour over the egg mixture and sprinkle with the cheese and cinnamon. Place on the rack and bake for 20 minutes until golden and set. You may need to cover the tops with a little kitchen foil if becoming too brown, and it may be necessary to cook these in two batches. Serve with the salad leaves.

Fish Puff Tart

Serves 4

350 g/12 oz prepared puff pastry,
thawed if frozen
150 g/5 oz smoked haddock
150 g/5 oz cod
1 tbsp pesto
2 tomatoes, sliced
125 g/4 oz goats' cheese, sliced
1 medium egg, beaten
freshly chopped parsley, to garnish

Fit the extender to the halogen oven bowl and place the low rack in the oven. Set the oven to 190˚C/375˚F. On a lightly floured surface, roll out the pastry into a 20.5 x 15 cm/8 x 6 inch rectangle. If this size does not fit, roll the pastry into a circle that fits.

Draw a 2.5 cm/1 inch border on the edge of the pastry with a knife. Be careful not to cut through the pastry. Lightly cut crisscross patterns in the border of the pastry.

Place the fish on a chopping board and, with a sharp knife, skin the smoked haddock and cod. Spread the pesto evenly over the bottom of the pastry case with the back of a spoon. Arrange the fish, tomatoes and cheese in the pastry case and brush the pastry with the beaten egg.

Place on the rack and bake the tart in the oven for 18–20 minutes until the pastry is well risen, puffed and golden brown. Garnish with the chopped parsley and serve immediately.

Smoked Mackerel Vol-au-Vents

Serves 4–6

350 g/12 oz prepared puff pastry
1 small egg, beaten
2 tsp sesame seeds
225 g/8 oz peppered smoked
mackerel, skinned and chopped
5 cm/2 inch piece cucumber
4 tbsp soft cream cheese
2 tbsp cranberry sauce
1 tbsp freshly chopped dill
1 tbsp finely grated lemon zest
dill sprigs, to garnish

Fit the extender to the halogen oven bowl and put the low rack in the oven. Set the oven to 190˚C/375˚F. Roll the pastry out on a lightly floured surface and, using a 9 cm/3¹/₂ inch fluted cutter, cut out 12 rounds.

Using a 1 cm/¹/₂ inch cutter, mark a lid in the centre of each round. Place on a damp baking sheet or 2 small trays and brush the pastry with a little beaten egg.

Sprinkle the pastry with the sesame seeds. Bake in the oven for 12–15 minutes until golden brown and well risen.

Remove from the oven and transfer the vol-au-vents to a chopping board. When cool enough to touch, carefully remove the lids with a small, sharp knife. Scoop out any uncooked pastry from the inside of each vol-au-vent, then return to the oven for 5–8 minutes to dry out. Remove and allow to cool.

Flake the mackerel into small pieces and reserve. Peel the cucumber if desired, cut into very small dice and add to the mackerel.

Beat the soft cream cheese with the cranberry sauce, dill and lemon zest. Stir in the mackerel and cucumber and use to fill the vol-au-vents. Place the lids on top and garnish with dill sprigs.

Olive Feta Parcels

Makes 6

1 small red pepper
1 small yellow pepper
125 g/4 oz assorted marinated
green and black olives
125 g/4 oz feta cheese
2 tbsp pine nuts, lightly toasted
6 sheets filo pastry
3 tbsp olive oil
sour cream and chive dip, to serve

Line the high rack with kitchen foil and place in the halogen oven. Set the oven to 190°C/375°F. Cut the peppers into quarters and remove the seeds. Place skin-side up on the foil-lined rack and switch the timer to 10 minutes. Cook, turning occasionally, for 10 minutes, or until the skins begin to blacken.

When ready, remove from the oven and place the peppers in a polythene bag and leave until cool enough to handle, then skin and thinly slice. Chop the olives and cut the feta cheese into small cubes. Mix together the olives, feta, sliced peppers and pine nuts.

Cut 1 sheet of filo pastry in half, then brush with a little of the oil. Place a spoonful of the olive and feta mix about one third of the way up the pastry. Fold over the pastry and wrap to form a square parcel which encases the filling. Place the parcel in the centre of the second half of the pastry sheet. Brush the edges lightly with a little oil, bring up the corners to meet in the centre and twist them loosely to form a purse.

Brush with a little more oil and repeat with the remaining filo pastry and filling. Cook in two batches if space is tight. Place the parcels on two lightly oiled, small ovenproof trays or plates. Place both racks in the oven if using 2 trays. Place a tray on each rack. Cook in the oven for 10–15 minutes until crisp and golden brown. Serve with the dip.

Coriander Chicken Soy Sauce Cakes

Serves 4

¹/₄ cucumber, peeled
1 shallot, peeled and thinly sliced
6 radishes, trimmed and sliced
350 g/12 oz skinless, boneless
chicken thigh
4 tbsp roughly chopped fresh
coriander
2 spring onions, trimmed and
roughly chopped
1 red chilli, deseeded and chopped
finely grated zest of ¹/₂ lime
2 tbsp soy sauce
1 tbsp caster sugar
2 tbsp rice vinegar
1 red chilli, deseeded and
finely sliced
freshly chopped coriander,
to garnish

Place the low rack in the halogen oven and set the oven to 190˚C/375˚F. Halve the cucumber lengthways, deseed and dice.

In a bowl, mix the shallot and radishes. Chill until ready to serve with the diced cucumber.

Place the chicken thighs in a food processor and blend until coarsely chopped. Add the coriander and spring onions to the chicken with the chilli, lime zest and soy sauce. Blend again until mixed.

Using slightly damp hands, shape the chicken mixture into 12 small rounds. Place the rounds on a lightly oiled baking tray or ovenproof plate. (You may need to do this in two batches). Close the lid and cook in the oven for 15 minutes, or until golden. Reserve.

Pour the sugar with 2 tablespoons water into a small saucepan and cook for 3 minutes, stirring. Increase the heat and then boil for 5–8 minutes until syrupy. Remove from the heat and allow to cool a little, then stir in the vinegar and chilli slices. Pour over the cucumber and the radish and shallot salad. Garnish with the chopped coriander and serve the chicken cakes with the salad immediately.

Cantonese Chicken Wings

Serves 6–8

3 tbsp hoisin sauce
2 tbsp dark soy sauce
1 tbsp sesame oil
1 garlic clove, peeled and crushed
2.5 cm/1 inch piece fresh root ginger, peeled and grated
1 tbsp Chinese rice wine or dry sherry
2 tsp chilli bean sauce
2 tsp red or white wine vinegar
2 tbsp soft light brown sugar
900 g/2 lb large chicken wings
50 g/2 oz cashew nuts, chopped
2 spring onions, trimmed and finely chopped

Place the low rack in the halogen oven and set the oven to 200˚C/400˚F. Place the hoisin sauce, soy sauce, sesame oil, garlic, ginger, Chinese rice wine or sherry, chilli bean sauce, vinegar and sugar in a medium saucepan with 6 tablespoons water. Bring to the boil and simmer for 10 minutes. Remove from the heat and leave to cool.

Place the chicken wings in a roasting tin or ovenproof dish, if possible in a single layer. If not possible, place in two layers and use the extender. Pour over the glaze and stir until the wings are coated thoroughly.

Cover the tin with kitchen foil, securing the foil around the rim. Place in the oven. Roast for 25–30 minutes until cooked. Remove the foil occasionally and baste the wings.

Reduce the oven temperature to 170˚C/325˚F. Turn the wings over and sprinkle with the chopped cashew nuts and spring onions. Return to the oven and cook for 5 minutes, or until the nuts are lightly browned, the glaze is sticky and the wings are very tender. Remove from the oven and leave to stand for 5 minutes before arranging on a warmed platter. Serve immediately with finger bowls and plenty of napkins.

Sweet & Sour Spareribs

Serves 6–8

1.6 kg/3¹/₂ lb pork spareribs
4 tbsp clear honey
1 tbsp Worcestershire sauce
1 tsp Chinese five-spice powder
4 tbsp soy sauce
2¹/₂ tbsp dry sherry
1 tsp chilli sauce
2 garlic cloves, peeled and chopped
1¹/₂ tbsp tomato purée
1 tsp dry mustard powder (optional)
spring onion curls, to garnish

Place the low rack in the halogen oven and set the oven to 200°C/400°F. If necessary, place the ribs on a chopping board and, using a sharp knife, cut the joint in between the ribs, to form single ribs. Place the ribs in a shallow dish in a single layer.

Spoon the honey, the Worcestershire sauce and the Chinese five-spice powder with the soy sauce, sherry and chilli sauce into a small saucepan and cook for 5 minutes. Remove from the heat and stir until smooth. Stir in the chopped garlic, the tomato purée and mustard powder, if using.

Pour the honey mixture over the ribs and spoon the marinade over until the ribs are coated evenly. Cover with clingfilm and leave to marinate in the refrigerator, preferably overnight, occasionally spooning the marinade over the ribs.

When ready to cook, remove the ribs from the marinade and place in a deeper dish (or two smaller dishes, then use both racks or cook in two batches.) Spoon over a little of the marinade and reserve the remainder. Place the spareribs on the low rack in the oven. Cook for 30–35 minutes until cooked and the outsides are crisp. If liked, baste occasionally with the reserved marinade during cooking. Garnish with a few spring onion curls and serve immediately.

Char Sui Pork Noodle Salad

Serves 4– 6

200 g/7 oz flat rice noodles
4 tbsp black treacle
2 tbsp dark soy sauce
3 tbsp Chinese rice wine or
dry sherry
3 star anise, roughly crushed
1 cinnamon stick
350 g/12 oz pork tenderloin,
in 1 piece
1 tbsp groundnut oil
2 garlic cloves, peeled and
finely chopped
1 tsp freshly grated root ginger
3 spring onions, trimmed and sliced
125 g/4 oz pak choi,
roughly chopped
2 tbsp light soy sauce
fresh coriander leaves, to garnish
plum sauce, to serve

Place the high rack in the halogen oven and set the oven to 200°C/400°F. Soak the noodles in boiling water according to the packet instructions. Drain and reserve. Place the treacle, soy sauce, Chinese rice wine or sherry, star anise and cinnamon stick in a small saucepan and heat for 5 minutes. Remove and stir until mixed thoroughly, then reserve.

Trim the pork tenderloin of any excess fat and put into a shallow dish. Pour the cooled sauce over the tenderloin. Turn the pork, making sure it is completely coated in the sauce. Place in the refrigerator and leave to marinate for 4 hours, turning occasionally. Remove the pork from its marinade and transfer to a roasting tin or ovenproof tray. Roast in the oven for 15–20 minutes, basting once, until the pork is cooked through. Remove from the oven and leave until just warm.

Heat the wok, add the oil, and when hot, add the garlic, ginger and spring onions. Stir-fry for 30 seconds before adding the pak choi. Stir-fry for a further 1 minute until the pak choi has wilted, then add the noodles and soy sauce. Toss for a few seconds until well mixed, then transfer to a large serving dish. Leave to cool.

Thickly slice the pork fillet and add to the cooled noodles. Garnish with coriander leaves and serve with plum sauce.

Cheese-crusted Potato Scones

Serves 6

200 g/7 oz self-raising flour
25 g/1 oz wholemeal flour
1/2 tsp salt
11/2 tsp baking powder
25 g/1 oz butter, cubed
5 tbsp milk
175 g/6 oz cold mashed potato
freshly ground black pepper

To finish:

2 tbsp milk
40 g/11/2 oz mature Cheddar
cheese, finely grated
paprika, to dust
basil sprig, to garnish

Fit the extender to the halogen oven bowl and place the high rack in the oven. Set the oven to 185°C/365°F. Sift the flours, salt and baking powder into a large bowl. Rub in the butter until the mixture resembles fine breadcrumbs.

Stir 4 tablespoons of the milk into the mashed potato and season with black pepper. Add the dry ingredients to the potato mixture, mixing together with a fork and adding the remaining 1 tablespoon of milk if needed.

Knead the dough on a lightly floured surface for a few seconds until smooth. Roll out to a 15 cm/6 inch round and transfer to an oiled baking sheet or tray.

Mark the scone round into six wedges, cutting about halfway through with a small, sharp knife. Brush with milk, then sprinkle with the cheese and a faint dusting of paprika. Bake in the oven for 12– 15 minutes until well risen and golden brown. Transfer to a wire rack and leave to cool for 5 minutes before breaking into wedges.

Serve warm or leave to cool completely. Once cool, store the scones in an airtight tin. Garnish with a sprig of basil and serve split and buttered.

Meat

Dishes

Halogen ovens are a great way of cooking this popular and important food group; with their evenly distributed heat and large capacity, they allow you to cook quantities big enough for all the family in less time than a traditional oven. Whether you like your meat tender or crispy, these recipes offer something for everyone. Try such classic favourites as Lancashire Hotpot and Lasagne, or branch out with tantalising new flavour combinations such as Roquefort, Parma & Rocket Pizza.

Lancashire Hotpot

Serves 4

1 kg/2¹/₄ lb middle end neck of lamb, divided into cutlets
2 tbsp vegetable oil
2 large onions, peeled and sliced
2 tsp plain flour
150 ml/¹/₄ pint vegetable or lamb stock
700 g/1¹/₂ lb waxy potatoes, peeled and thickly sliced
salt and freshly ground black pepper
1 bay leaf
2 fresh thyme sprigs
1 tbsp melted butter
2 tbsp freshly chopped herbs, to garnish
freshly cooked green beans, to serve

Fit the extender to the halogen oven bowl and set the oven to 190˚C/375˚F. Trim any excess fat from the lamb cutlets. Heat the oil in a frying pan and brown the cutlets in batches for 3–4 minutes. Remove with a slotted spoon and reserve.

Add the onions to the frying pan and cook for 6–8 minutes until softened and just beginning to colour. Stir in the flour and cook for a few seconds, then gradually pour in the stock, stirring well, and bring to the boil. Remove from the heat.

Spread the base of a large casserole dish (check it will fit in the oven) with half the potato slices. Top with half the onions and season well with salt and pepper. Arrange the browned meat in a layer. Season again and add the remaining onions, bay leaf and thyme. Pour in the remaining liquid from the onions and top with remaining potatoes so that they overlap in a single layer. Brush the potatoes with the melted butter and season again.

Switch the timer to 60 minutes, cover with the lid and cook. When the timer buzzes, remove the lid from the casserole and continue to cook for 20–30 minutes until the potatoes are brown. Garnish with chopped herbs and serve immediately with green beans.

Lasagne

Serves 4

450 g/1 lb lean minced beef steak

1 large onion, peeled and chopped

2 celery stalks, trimmed and chopped

125 g/4 oz button mushrooms, wiped and chopped

5 tbsp plain flour

2 garlic cloves, peeled and chopped

300 ml/1/2 pint beef stock

1 tbsp freeze-dried mixed herbs

5 tbsp tomato purée

salt and freshly ground black pepper

75 g/3 oz butter

750 ml/1 $^1/_4$ pints milk

1 tsp wholegrain mustard

$^1/_4$ tsp freshly grated nutmeg

9 lasagne sheets

75g/3oz freshly grated Parmesan cheese

freshly chopped parsley, to garnish

Fit the extender to the halogen oven bowl and place the low rack in the oven. Set the oven to 200°C/400°F.

Make the Bologenese sauce. Cook the beef in a large saucepan for 10 minutes, stirring to break up lumps. Add the onion, celery and mushrooms and cook for 4 minutes, or until softened slightly. Stir in the garlic and 1 tbsp of the flour; cook for 1 minute. Stir in the stock, herbs and tomato purée. Season to taste. Bring to the boil, then cover, reduce the heat and simmer for 45 minutes.

Melt the butter in a small, heavy-based pan, add 4 tbsp flour and cook gently, stirring, for 2 minutes. Remove from the heat and gradually stir in the milk. Return to the heat and cook, stirring, for 2 minutes, or until the sauce thickens. Bring to the boil, remove from the heat and stir in the mustard. Season to taste with salt, pepper and nutmeg.

Butter an ovenproof dish and spread a thin layer of the white sauce over the base. Cover completely with 3 sheets of lasagne. Spoon a quarter of the Bolognese sauce over the lasagne. Spoon over a quarter of the remaining white sauce, then sprinkle with a quarter of the cheese. Repeat the layers. Bake in the oven for 30 minutes, or until golden brown. Garnish with chopped parsley.

Leg of Lamb with Minted Rice

Serves 6

1 tbsp olive oil
1 medium onion, peeled and
finely chopped
1 garlic clove, peeled and crushed
1 celery stalk, trimmed and chopped
1 large, mild red chilli, deseeded
and chopped
75 g/3 oz long-grain rice
150 ml/¼ pint lamb or chicken stock
2 tbsp freshly chopped mint
salt and freshly ground black pepper
1.4 kg/3 lb boned leg of lamb
freshly cooked vegetables, to serve

Fit the extender to the halogen oven bowl and put the low rack in the oven. Set the oven to 180°C/350°F. Heat the oil in a frying pan and gently cook the onion for 5 minutes. Stir in the garlic, celery and chilli and continue to cook for 3–4 minutes.

Place the rice and the stock in a large saucepan and cook, covered, for 10–12 minutes until the rice is tender and all the liquid is absorbed. Stir in the onion and celery mixture, then leave to cool. Once the rice mixture is cold, stir in the chopped mint and season to taste with salt and pepper.

Place the boned lamb skin-side down and spoon the rice mixture along the centre of the meat. Roll up the meat to enclose the stuffing and tie securely with string. Place in a roasting tin or line the rack with kitchen foil and place the lamb on the rack. Roast in the oven for 1 hour 20 minutes, or until cooked to personal preference. Remove from the oven and leave to rest in a warm place for 10 minutes before carving. Serve with a selection of cooked vegetables.

Roasted Lamb with Rosemary

Serves 6

1.4 kg/3 lb leg of lamb
6 garlic cloves, peeled
few fresh rosemary sprigs, plus extra
to garnish
salt and freshly ground black pepper
4 slices pancetta
4 tbsp olive oil
4 tbsp red wine vinegar
675 g/1¹/₂ lb potatoes
1 large onion
freshly cooked ratatouille, to serve

Fit the extender to the halogen oven bowl and place the low rack in the oven. Set the oven to 200°C/400°F. Wipe the leg of lamb with a clean, damp cloth, then with a sharp knife, make small, deep incisions into the meat. Cut 2–3 garlic cloves into small slivers, then insert with a few small sprigs of rosemary into the lamb. Season to taste with salt and pepper and cover the lamb with the slices of pancetta.

Drizzle over 1 tablespoon of the olive oil and lay a few more rosemary sprigs across the lamb. Either line the rack with kitchen foil and place the lamb on the rack, or use an ovenproof dish that will fit in the oven. Roast in the oven for 30 minutes, then pour over the vinegar.

Peel the potatoes and cut into large dice. Peel the onion and cut into thick wedges, then thickly slice the remaining garlic. Arrange around the lamb. It will not matter if the vegetables do not all fit in the dish – if they tumble on the oven floor, that is fine. Pour the remaining olive oil over the potatoes, then continue to roast for a further 1 hour, or until the lamb is tender. Garnish with fresh sprigs of rosemary and serve immediately with the roast potatoes and ratatouille.

Pork Chop Hotpot

Serves 4

4 pork chops
flour for dusting
225 g/8 oz shallots, peeled
2 garlic cloves, peeled
50 g/2 oz sun-dried tomatoes
2 tbsp olive oil
400 g can plum tomatoes
150 ml/¼ pint red wine
150 ml/¼ pint chicken stock
3 tbsp tomato purée
2 tbsp freshly chopped oregano
salt and freshly ground black pepper
fresh oregano leaves, to garnish

To serve:

freshly cooked new potatoes
French beans

Fit the extender to the halogen oven bowl and place the low rack in the oven. Set the oven to 190°C/375°F. Trim the pork chops, removing any excess fat, wipe with a clean, damp cloth, then dust with a little flour and reserve. Cut the shallots in half if large. Chop the garlic and slice the sun-dried tomatoes.

Heat the olive oil in an ovenproof dish and cook the pork chops for about 5 minutes, turning occasionally during cooking, until browned all over. Using a slotted spoon, carefully lift out of the dish and reserve. Add the shallots and cook for 5 minutes, stirring occasionally.

Return the pork chops to the dish and scatter with the garlic and sun-dried tomatoes, then pour over the can of tomatoes with their juice.

Blend the red wine, stock and tomato purée together and add the chopped oregano. Season to taste with salt and pepper, then pour over the pork chops and bring to a gentle boil. Cover with a close-fitting lid. Cook in the oven for 30 minutes, or until the pork chops are tender. Adjust the seasoning to taste, then scatter with a few oregano leaves and serve immediately with freshly cooked potatoes and French beans.

Roasted Vegetables Sausages

Serves 4

2 medium aubergines, trimmed
3 medium courgettes, trimmed
4 tbsp olive oil
6 garlic cloves
8 Tuscany-style sausages
4 plum tomatoes
2 x 300 g cans cannellini beans
salt and freshly ground black pepper
1 bunch fresh basil, roughly torn
4 tbsp Parmesan cheese, grated

Fit the extender to the halogen oven bowl and place the low rack in the oven. Set the oven to 200˚C/400˚F. Cut the aubergines and courgettes into bite-sized chunks. Place the olive oil in a roasting tin or ovenproof dish and heat on the hob for 3 minutes, or until very hot. Add the aubergines, courgettes and garlic cloves, then stir until coated in the hot oil. Place on the rack and close the lid. Cook for 10 minutes, then remove from the oven and stir.

Lightly prick the sausages, add to the vegetables and return to the oven. Close the lid and continue to roast for a further 20 minutes, turning once during cooking, until the vegetables are tender and the sausages are golden brown.

Meanwhile, roughly chop the plum tomatoes and drain the cannellini beans. Remove the sausages from the oven and stir in the tomatoes and cannellini beans. Season to taste with salt and pepper, then return to the oven for 5 minutes, or until heated thoroughly.

Scatter over the basil leaves and sprinkle with plenty of Parmesan cheese and extra freshly ground black pepper. Serve immediately.

Roast Cured Pork Loin

Serves 4

2 tbsp wholegrain mustard
2 tbsp clear honey
1 tsp coarsely crushed black pepper
900 g/2 lb piece smoked cured pork loin
675 g1¹/₂ lb potatoes, peeled and
thinly sliced
75 g/3 oz butter, diced
1 large onion, peeled and finely chopped
25 g/1 oz plain flour
salt and freshly ground black pepper
600 ml/1 pint milk
fresh green salad, to serve

Fit the extender to the halogen oven bowl and place the low and high racks in the oven. Set the oven to 200°C/400°F. Mix together the mustard, honey and black pepper. Spread evenly over the pork loin. Place in the centre of a large square of kitchen foil, wrap loosely and reserve. Calculate the cooking time, allowing 15 minutes per 450 g/1 lb, plus an extra 15 minutes (45 minutes in total).

Meanwhile, layer one third of the potatoes, one third of the butter, half the onion and half the flour in a gratin or ovenproof dish. Add half the remaining potatoes and butter and the remaining onions and flour. Finally, cover with the remaining potatoes. Season well with salt and pepper between layers. Pour in the milk and dot with the remaining butter. Cover the dish loosely with kitchen foil and put in the oven on the low rack. Cook for 1¹/₄ hours.

After cooking the potatoes for 30 minutes, place the wrapped pork on the high rack and close the lid. Cook for 45 minutes, unwrapping the joint for the last 30 minutes of cooking time. Test that the pork is cooked. If juices run pink, cook for a further 15 minutes. Remove the pork loin from the oven and leave to rest in a warm place for 15 minutes before carving thinly.

Remove the kitchen foil from the potatoes and cook for a further 20 minutes until tender and golden. Serve with the potatoes and a fresh green salad.

Shepherd's Pie

Serves 4

2 tbsp vegetable or olive oil
1 onion, peeled and finely chopped
1 carrot, peeled and finely chopped
1 celery stalk, trimmed and
finely chopped
1 tbsp fresh thyme sprigs
450 g/1 lb leftover roast lamb,
finely chopped
150 ml/¼ pint red wine
150 ml/¼ pint lamb or vegetable
stock or leftover gravy
2 tbsp tomato purée
salt and freshly ground black pepper
700 g/1½ lb potatoes, peeled and
cut into chunks
25 g/1 oz butter
6 tbsp milk
1 tbsp freshly chopped parsley
fresh herbs, to garnish

Fit the extender to the halogen oven bowl and place the low rack in the oven. Set the oven to 200˚C/400˚F. Heat the oil in an ovenproof dish and add the onion, carrot and celery. Cook over a medium heat for 8–10 minutes until softened and starting to brown.

Add the thyme and cook briefly, then add the cooked lamb, wine, stock or gravy and tomato purée. Season to taste with salt and pepper and cook for 15 minutes, or until reduced and thickened. Remove from the oven to cool slightly and season again.

Meanwhile, boil the potatoes in plenty of salted water for 12–15 minutes until tender. Drain and return to the saucepan over a low heat to dry out. Remove from the heat and add the butter, milk and parsley. Mash until creamy, adding a little more milk if necessary. Adjust the seasoning.

Transfer the lamb mixture to an ovenproof dish and replace the low rack for the high rack. Spoon the mash over the filling and spread evenly to cover completely. Fork the surface, place on a baking sheet, then cook in the oven for 20–25 minutes until the potato topping is browned and the filling is piping hot. Garnish and serve.

Italian Beef Pot Roast

Serves 6

1.8 kg/4 lb brisket of beef
225 g/8 oz small onions, peeled
3 garlic cloves, peeled and chopped
2 celery stalks, trimmed
and chopped
2 carrots, peeled and sliced
450 g/1 lb ripe tomatoes
300 ml/¹/₂ pint Italian red wine
2 tbsp olive oil
300 ml/¹/₂ pint beef stock
1 tbsp tomato purée
2 tsp dried mixed herbs
salt and freshly ground black pepper
25 g/1 oz butter
25 g/1 oz plain flour
freshly cooked vegetables, to serve

Fit the extender to the halogen oven bowl and place the low rack in the oven. Set the oven to 170˚C/325˚F. Place the beef in a bowl. Add the onions, garlic, celery and carrots. Place the tomatoes in a bowl and cover with boiling water. Allow to stand for 2 minutes, then drain. Peel away the skins, discard the seeds and chop, then add to the bowl with the red wine. Cover tightly and marinate in the refrigerator overnight.

Lift the marinated beef from the bowl and pat dry with absorbent kitchen paper. Heat the olive oil in a frying pan, then brown the beef all over. Place in an ovenproof dish or casserole dish. Drain the vegetables from the marinade, reserving the marinade. Add the vegetables to the frying pan and fry gently for 5 minutes, stirring occasionally, until all the vegetables are browned.

Add the vegetables to the ovenproof dish or casserole dish, then add the marinade, beef stock, tomato purée, mixed herbs and season with salt and pepper. Bring to the boil, cover and cook in the oven for 2–2¹/₂ hours.

Using a slotted spoon, transfer the beef and any large vegetables to a plate and leave in a warm place. Blend the butter and flour to form a paste. Bring the casserole juices to the boil and then gradually stir in small spoonfuls of the paste. Cook until thickened. Serve with the sauce and a selection of vegetables.

Normandy Pork

Serves 4

575 g/1¹/₄ lb lean pork
2 tbsp olive oil
2 medium onions, peeled and sliced
2–3 garlic cloves, peeled and chopped
2 celery stalks, trimmed and sliced
1 red pepper, deseeded and chopped
1 cooking apple, peeled, cored and cubed
2 tbsp plain flour
300 ml/¹/₂ pint cider or apple juice
450 ml/³/₄ pint pork or chicken stock
salt and freshly ground black pepper
few fresh sage sprigs
1 red apple, cored and cut into wedges, to garnish (optional)
boiled potatoes, mashed with melted butter and chopped spring onions, apple and red cabbage, to serve

Fit the extender to the halogen oven bowl and place the low rack in the oven. Set the oven to 190°C/375°F. Trim the pork, discarding any fat, then cut into small pieces. Heat the oil in a frying pan and fry the pork over a medium heat on all sides for 5–8 minutes until sealed. Remove from the pan using a slotted spoon.

Add all the vegetables and the cooking apple to the oil remaining in the pan and fry for 8–10 minutes until the vegetables are beginning to soften. Remove and place in a casserole dish or ovenproof dish.

Sprinkle in the flour and cook for 2 minutes, then remove the pan from the heat and gradually stir in the cider or apple juice and then the stock. Return to the heat and bring to the boil, stirring occasionally. Season to taste and add the sage sprigs. Transfer to the casserole dish.

Cover and place on the rack, close the lid and cook for 1 hour. Adjust the seasoning, stir in the apple wedges, if using, and cook for a further 10–15 minutes until the pork is tender. Serve with freshly cooked mashed potatoes with melted butter and chopped spring onions, apple and red cabbage.

Grilled Steaks Saffron Potatoes

Serves 4

700 g/1¹/₂ lb new potatoes, halved
few saffron strands
300 ml/¹/₂ pint vegetable or
beef stock
1 small onion, peeled and
finely chopped
25 g/1 oz butter
salt and freshly ground black pepper
2 tsp balsamic vinegar
2 tbsp olive oil
1 tsp caster sugar
8 plum tomatoes, halved
4 sirloin steaks, each
weighing 225 g/8 oz
2 tbsp freshly chopped parsley

Cook the potatoes in boiling salted water for 8 minutes and drain well. Return the potatoes to the saucepan along with the saffron, stock, onion and butter. Season to taste with salt and pepper and simmer, uncovered, for 10 minutes until the potatoes are tender.

Meanwhile, place the high rack in the halogen oven and set the oven to 200°C/400°F. If liked, cover the rack with kitchen foil. Mix together the vinegar, olive oil, sugar and seasoning. Arrange the tomatoes cut-side up on the rack and drizzle over the dressing. Cook for 5–8 minutes, basting occasionally, until tender and keep warm.

Place the steaks on the rack and cook for 8–12 minutes until cooked to personal preference and depending on thickness.

Arrange the potatoes and tomatoes in the centre of four serving plates. Top with the steaks. Sprinkle over the parsley and serve immediately.

Crown Roast of Lamb

Serves 6

1 prepared crown roast of lamb
salt and freshly ground black pepper
1 tbsp sunflower oil
1 small onion, peeled and
finely chopped
2–3 garlic cloves, peeled
and crushed
2 celery stalks, trimmed and
finely chopped
125 g/4 oz cooked mixed basmati
and wild rice
75 g/3 oz ready-to-eat-dried
apricots, chopped
50 g/2 oz pine nuts, toasted
1 tbsp finely grated orange zest
2 tbsp freshly chopped coriander
1 small egg, beaten
freshly roasted potatoes and green
vegetables, to serve

Fit the extender to the halogen oven bowl and place the low rack in the oven. Set the oven to 190°C/375°F. Wipe the crown roast and season the cavity with salt and pepper. Place in a roasting tin and cover the ends of the bones with small pieces of kitchen foil.

Heat the oil in a small saucepan and cook the onion, garlic and celery for 5 minutes, then remove the saucepan from the heat. Add the cooked rice with the apricots, pine nuts, orange zest and coriander. Season with salt and pepper, then stir in the egg and mix well.

Carefully spoon the prepared stuffing into the cavity of the lamb and place some kitchen foil over the stuffing Close the oven lid and cook for 1¼ hours. Remove the lamb from the oven and remove and discard the kitchen foil from on top of the stuffing and the bones. Return to the oven and continue to cook for a further 15 minutes, or until cooked to personal preference.

Remove from the oven and rest in a warm place for 10 minutes before serving with the roast potatoes and freshly cooked vegetables.

Hot Salami Vegetable Gratin

Serves 4

350 g/12 oz carrots
175 g/6 oz fine green beans
250 g/9 oz asparagus tips
175 g/6 oz frozen peas
225 g/8 oz Italian salami
1 tbsp olive oil
1 tbsp freshly chopped mint
25 g/1 oz butter
150 g/5 oz baby spinach leaves
150 ml/¼ pint double cream
salt and freshly ground black pepper
1 small or ½ whole olive ciabatta loaf
75 g/3 oz Parmesan cheese, grated
green salad, to serve

Place the low rack in the halogen oven and set the oven to 200˚C/400˚F. Peel and slice the carrots, trim the beans and asparagus and reserve. Cook the carrots in a saucepan of lightly salted boiling water for 10 minutes. Add the remaining vegetables, except the spinach, and cook for a further 5 minutes, or until tender. Drain and place in an ovenproof dish that will fit in the oven.

Discard any skin from the outside of the salami, if necessary, then chop roughly. Heat the oil in a frying pan and fry the salami for 4–5 minutes, stirring occasionally, until golden. Using a slotted spoon, transfer the salami to the ovenproof dish and scatter over the mint.

Add the butter to the frying pan and cook the spinach for 1–2 minutes until just wilted. Stir in the double cream and season well with salt and pepper. Spoon the mixture over the vegetables.

Whizz the ciabatta loaf in a food processor to make breadcrumbs. Stir in the Parmesan cheese and sprinkle over the vegetables. Place on the rack, close the lid and bake in the oven for 20–25 minutes until golden and heated through. Serve with a green salad.

Antipasto Penne

Serves 4

3 medium courgettes, trimmed
4 plum tomatoes
175 g/6 oz Italian ham
2 tbsp olive oil
salt and freshly ground
black pepper
350 g/12 oz dried penne pasta
285 g jar antipasto
125 g/4 oz mozzarella cheese,
drained and diced
125 g/4 oz Gorgonzola
cheese, crumbled
3 tbsp freshly chopped
flat-leaf parsley

Place the low rack in the halogen oven and set the oven to 190°C/375°F. Cut the courgettes into thick slices. Rinse the tomatoes and cut into quarters, then cut the ham into strips.

Pour the oil into a large saucepan and heat for 1 minute. Remove from the heat and stir in the courgettes. Cook for 6 minutes. Add the tomatoes and cook for a further 3 minutes. Add the ham to the dish and cook for 4 minutes until all the vegetables are charred and the ham is brown. Season to taste with salt and pepper.

Meanwhile, plunge the pasta into a large saucepan of lightly salted, boiling water, return to a rolling boil, stir and cook for 8 minutes, or until *al dente*. Drain well and return to the saucepan.

Stir the antipasto into the vegetables and add the cooked pasta. Spoon into an ovenproof dish. Toss together gently with the remaining ingredients. Cook in the oven for 15 minutes and serve immediately.

Cannelloni

Serves 4

2 tbsp olive oil
175 g/6 oz fresh pork mince
75 g/3 oz chicken livers, chopped
1 small onion, peeled and chopped
1 garlic clove, peeled and chopped
175 g/6 oz frozen chopped
spinach, thawed
1 tbsp freeze-dried oregano
pinch freshly grated nutmeg
salt and freshly ground black pepper
175 g/6 oz ricotta cheese
25 g/1 oz butter
25 g/1 oz plain flour
600 ml/1 pint milk
600 ml/1 pint ready-made
tomato sauce
16 precooked cannelloni tubes
50 g/2 oz Parmesan cheese, grated
green salad, to serve

Place the low rack in the halogen oven and set the oven to 190˚C/375˚F. Heat the olive oil in a frying pan and cook the mince and chicken livers for about 5 minutes, stirring occasionally, until browned all over. Break up any lumps if necessary with a wooden spoon.

Add the onion and garlic and cook for 4 minutes, or until softened. Add the spinach, oregano, nutmeg and season to taste with salt and pepper. Cook until all the liquid has evaporated, then remove the pan from the heat and allow to cool. Stir in the ricotta cheese.

Meanwhile, melt the butter in a small saucepan and stir in the plain flour to form a roux. Cook for 2 minutes, stirring occasionally. Remove from the heat and blend in the milk until smooth. Return to the heat and bring to the boil, stirring, until the sauce has thickened. Reserve.

Spoon a thin layer of the tomato sauce on the base of an ovenproof dish that fits in the oven. Stuff the pork filling into the cannelloni tubes. Arrange on top of the tomato sauce. Spoon over the remaining sauce.

Pour over the white sauce and sprinkle with the Parmesan cheese. Place on the rack and cook in the oven for 25–30 minutes until the cannelloni is tender and the top is golden brown. Serve immediately with a green salad.

Tagliatelle with Spicy Sausage Ragù

Serves 4

3 tbsp olive oil
6 spicy sausages
1 small onion, peeled and
finely chopped
1 tsp fennel seeds
175 g/6 oz fresh pork mince
225 g can chopped tomatoes
with garlic
1 tbsp sun-dried tomato paste
2 tbsp red wine or port
salt and freshly ground
black pepper
350 g/12 oz tagliatelle
300 ml/¹/₂ pint prepared white
sauce (*see* page 68)
50 g/2 oz freshly grated
Parmesan cheese

Place the low rack in the halogen oven and set the oven to 200°C/400°F. Pour 1 tablespoon of the olive oil into an ovenproof dish. Prick the sausages, then add to the dish. Place in the oven and cook for 8–10 minutes until browned and cooked through. Remove and cut into thin diagonal slices. Reserve.

Pour the remaining olive oil into the dish and add the onion. Return to the oven and cook for 8–10 minutes until softened. Add the fennel seeds and pork mince and cook, stirring, for 5–8 minutes, or until the meat is sealed and browned. Switch the oven to 175°C/350°F. Stir in the tomatoes, tomato paste and the wine or port. Season to taste with salt and pepper. Stir, then return to the oven and cook for 30 minutes, covered.

Bring a large pan of lightly salted water to a rolling boil. Add the pasta and cook according to the packet instructions, or until *al dente*. Drain thoroughly and toss with the meat sauce.

Place half the pasta in an ovenproof dish, and cover with 4 tablespoons of the white sauce. Top with half the sausages and grated Parmesan cheese. Repeat the layering, finishing with white sauce and Parmesan cheese. Put on the rack and cook for 20 minutes, or until golden brown. Serve immediately.

Gnocchi ✺ Parma Ham Bake

Serves 4

3 tbsp olive oil
1 red onion, peeled and sliced
2 garlic cloves, peeled
175 g/6 oz plum tomatoes, skinned
and quartered
2 tbsp sun-dried tomato paste
250 g tub mascarpone cheese
salt and freshly ground
black pepper
1 tbsp freshly chopped tarragon
300 g/11 oz fresh gnocchi
125 g/4 oz Cheddar or Parmesan
cheese, grated
50 g/2 oz fresh white breadcrumbs
50 g/2 oz Parma ham, sliced
10 pitted green olives, halved
flat-leaf parsley sprigs. to garnish

Place the low rack in the halogen oven and set the oven to 180°C/350°F. Heat 2 tablespoons of the olive oil in a large frying pan and cook the onion and garlic for 5 minutes, or until softened. Stir in the tomatoes, sun-dried tomato paste and mascarpone cheese. Season to taste with salt and pepper. Add half the tarragon. Bring to the boil, then lower the heat immediately and simmer for 5 minutes.

Meanwhile, bring 1.7 litres/3 pints water to the boil in a large pan. Add the remaining olive oil and a good pinch of salt. Add the gnocchi and cook for 1–2 minutes until they rise to the surface.

Drain the gnocchi thoroughly and transfer to an ovenproof dish that fits in the oven bowl. Add the tomato sauce and toss gently to coat the pasta. Combine the Cheddar or Parmesan cheese with the breadcrumbs and remaining tarragon and scatter over the pasta mixture. Top with the Parma ham and olives and season again.

Place on the rack covered with kitchen foil. Cook in the oven for 20–25 minutes until golden and bubbling. Serve immediately, garnished with parsley sprigs.

Roquefort, Parma & Rocket Pizza

Serves 2–4

For the pizza dough:
225 g/8 oz strong plain flour
1/2 tsp salt
1/4 tsp quick-acting dried yeast
150 ml/1/4 pint warm water
1 tbsp extra virgin olive oil

For the tomato sauce:
400 g can chopped tomatoes
2 garlic cloves, peeled and crushed
grated zest of 1/2 lime
2 tbsp extra virgin olive oil
2 tbsp freshly chopped basil
1/2 tsp sugar
salt and freshly ground black pepper

For the topping:
125 g/4 oz Roquefort cheese, cut into chunks
6 slices Parma ham
50 g/2 oz rocket leaves, rinsed
1 tbsp extra virgin olive oil
50 g/2 oz Parmesan cheese, shaved

Place the high rack in the halogen oven and set the oven to 220°C/425°F.

Sift the flour and salt into a bowl and stir in the yeast. Make a well in the centre and gradually add the water and oil to form a soft dough.

Knead the dough on a floured surface for about 5 minutes until smooth and elastic. Place in a lightly oiled bowl and cover with cling film. Leave to rise in a warm place for 1 hour.

Knock the pizza dough with your fist a few times, shape and roll out on a lightly floured board to form a 25.5 cm/10 inch round. Place a baking tray or ovenproof dish in the oven and switch the timer to 2 minutes.

Place all of the sauce ingredients in an ovenproof dish and cover with foil. Cook in the oven for 15–20 minutes until the sauce has thickened and reduced by half. Spoon the tomato sauce over the shaped pizza dough. Place on the hot baking sheet and bake for 10 minutes.

Remove the pizza from the oven and top with the Roquefort and Parma ham, then bake for a further 10 minutes. Toss the rocket in the olive oil and pile onto the pizza. Sprinkle with the Parmesan cheese and serve immediately.

Hoisin Pork

Serves 4

1.4 kg/3 lb piece lean belly
pork, boned
sea salt
2 tsp Chinese five-spice powder
2 garlic cloves, peeled
and chopped
1 tsp sesame oil
4 tbsp hoisin sauce
1 tbsp clear honey
assorted salad leaves, to garnish

Fit the extender to the halogen oven bowl and place the low rack in the oven. Set the oven to 190˚C/375˚F. Using a sharp knife, cut the pork skin in a crisscross pattern, making sure not to cut all the way through into the flesh. Rub the salt evenly over the skin and leave to stand for 30 minutes.

Meanwhile, mix together the five spice powder, garlic, sesame oil, hoisin sauce and honey until smooth. Rub the mixture evenly over the pork skin. Place the pork on a plate and chill in the refrigerator to marinate for up to 6 hours.

Place the pork on a wire rack that fits inside a roasting tin or ovenproof dish. Roast the pork in the oven for 1–1¼ hours until the pork is very crisp and the juices run clear when pierced with a skewer.

Remove the pork from the heat, leave to rest for 15 minutes, then cut into strips. Arrange on a warmed serving platter. Garnish with salad leaves and serve immediately.

Individual Beef en Croute

Serves 4

4 pieces fillet steak, about 125 g/
4 oz each
2 tbsp olive oil
2–3 shallots, depending on size,
peeled and sliced
1 small red pepper, deseeded
and sliced
50 g/2 oz button mushrooms, wiped
and sliced
salt and freshly ground black pepper
flour, for dusting
450 g/1 lb prepared puff pastry
1 small egg, beaten
freshly cooked potatoes and
seasonal vegetables, to serve

Fit the extender to the halogen oven bowl and set the oven to 200°C/400°F. Place the steaks between two sheets of baking parchment and beat lightly with a meat mallet or rolling pin. Heat 2 teaspoons of the oil in a frying pan and, when hot, add the meat. Cook on both sides for about 1–2 minutes until sealed. Remove and place on kitchen paper and reserve in a cool place.

Heat the remaining oil in a saucepan and fry the shallots, red pepper and mushrooms for 5 minutes, or until softened. Remove and drain off any excess liquid. Season to taste.

Roll the pastry out on a lightly floured surface and cut into four rectangles, each about 20.5 x 25.5 cm/8 x 10 inches. Divide the mushroom mixture into four and place in the centre of each pastry rectangle. Place the meat on top. Brush the edges with a little beaten egg. Fold the pastry over to completely encase the meat and mushrooms and carefully seal, pressing the edges firmly together. Turn over and place on a lightly oiled baking sheet or ovenproof tray. Use any pastry trimmings to decorate the top. Brush with beaten egg.

Cook in the oven for 15–25 minutes until the pastry is well risen and is golden brown and depending on how rare you like your beef. Serve with freshly cooked potatoes and seasonal vegetables.

Poultry

❧ Game

Poultry & game form the tasty base for the huge array of dishes showcased in this chapter. Turkey Tetrazzini is a great choice for a simple weekday supper, whilst Pheasant with Sage & Blueberries makes a stunning dinner party showstopper. When it comes to roasting a chicken to perfection, the halogen oven really comes into its own; try Slow Roast Chicken with Oregano for a delicious yet hassle-free meal.

Chicken Ham Pie

Serves 6

1 tbsp olive oil
1 leek, trimmed and sliced
175 g/6 oz piece bacon, cut into
small dice
225 g/8 oz cooked skinless,
boneless chicken meat
2 avocados, peeled, pitted
and chopped
1 tbsp lemon juice
salt and freshly ground
black pepper
2 quantities of shortcrust pastry
(*see* page 156)
2 large eggs, beaten
150 ml/¼ pint natural yogurt
4 tbsp chicken stock
1 tbsp poppy seeds

To serve:

sliced red onion
mixed salad leaves

Fit the extender to the halogen oven and put the low rack in the oven. Set the oven to 180°C/350°F. Pour the oil into an ovenproof bowl and add the leek and bacon, then stir. Cook the leek and bacon for 5 minutes until soft but not coloured. Remove from the oven and place in a clean bowl, reserve.

Cut the chicken into bite-size pieces and add to the leek and bacon. Toss the avocados in the lemon juice, add to the chicken and season to taste with salt and pepper. Roll out half the pastry on a lightly floured surface and use to line an 18 cm/7 inch loose-bottomed, deep flan tin. Scoop the chicken mixture into the pastry case.

Mix together 1 egg, the yogurt and the chicken stock. Pour the yogurt mixture over the chicken. Roll out the remaining pastry on a lightly floured surface, and cut out the lid to 5 mm/¼ inch wider than the dish. Brush the rim with the remaining beaten egg and lay the pastry lid on top, pressing to seal. Knock the edges with the back of a knife to seal further. Cut a slit in the lid and brush with the egg.

Sprinkle with the poppy seeds, set the temperature to 190°C/375°F and switch the timer to 20 minutes. Place the pie on the rack and close the lid. Bake in the oven until the pastry is golden brown. You may need to increase the cooking time or cover the top with kitchen foil if browning too much. Serve with the onion and mixed salad leaves.

Slow Roast Chicken with Oregano

Serves 4–6

1.4 kg/3 lb oven-ready chicken,
preferably free range
1 lemon, halved
1 onion, peeled and quartered
50 g/2 oz butter, softened
salt and freshly ground
black pepper
1 kg/2¼ lb potatoes, peeled and
cut into chunks
1–2 tbsp virgin olive oil
1 tbsp dried oregano, crumbled
1 tsp fresh thyme leaves
2 tbsp freshly chopped thyme
fresh sage leaves, to garnish

Fit the extender to the halogen oven and place both racks in the oven. Set the oven to 200°C/400°F. Rinse the chicken and dry well, inside and out, with absorbent kitchen paper. Rub the chicken all over with the lemon halves, then squeeze the juice over it and into the cavity. Put the halves into the chicken cavity with the quartered onion. Rub the softened butter all over the chicken and season to taste with salt and pepper.

Toss the potatoes in the oil, season with salt and pepper, then add the dried oregano and fresh thyme. Put the potatoes in a small roasting tin or ovenproof dish. Place on the low rack and put the chicken on the high rack. Roast in the oven for 25 minutes. Reduce the oven temperature to 190°C/375°F. Turn the potatoes, sprinkle over half the fresh herbs and baste the chicken and potatoes with the juices. Continue roasting for 1 hour, or until the chicken is cooked, basting occasionally. The chicken is done when the juices run clear when the thigh is pierced with a skewer.

Transfer the chicken to a carving board, cover with kitchen foil and allow to rest for 10 minutes. Return the potatoes to the oven while the chicken is resting.

Carve the chicken into serving pieces and arrange on a large, heatproof serving dish. Arrange the potatoes around the chicken and drizzle over any remaining juices. Sprinkle with the remaining herbs and serve.

Creamy Turkey Tomato Pasta

Serves 4

4 tbsp olive oil
450 g/1 lb fresh turkey breasts, cut
into bite-size pieces
550 g/1 lb 3 oz cherry tomatoes,
on the vine
2 garlic cloves, peeled and chopped
4 tbsp balsamic vinegar
4 tbsp freshly shredded basil
salt and freshly ground black pepper
350 g/12 oz tagliatelle
200 ml tub crème fraîche
shaved Parmesan cheese, to garnish

Place the low rack in the halogen oven and set the oven to 200°C/400°F. Pour 2 tablespoons of the olive oil into a medium saucepan. Add the turkey, stir and cover with the lid. Cook for 5 minutes, or until sealed.

Add the remaining olive oil, the vine tomatoes, garlic and balsamic vinegar. Stir well and season to taste with salt and pepper. Spoon into an ovenproof dish, cover and cook in the oven for 30 minutes, or until the turkey is tender, and stir once during cooking.

Meanwhile, bring a large pan of lightly salted water to a rolling boil. Add the pasta and cook according to the packet instructions, or until *al dente*. Drain, return to the pan and keep warm. Stir the basil seasoning and crème fraîche into the cooked pasta.

Remove the cooked turkey and tomatoes from the oven and discard the vines. Stir the tomato mixture into the pasta and toss lightly together.

Tip into a warmed serving dish. Garnish with Parmesan cheese shavings and serve immediately.

Baked Thai Chicken Wings

Serves 4

4 tbsp clear honey
1 tbsp chilli sauce
1 garlic clove, peeled and crushed
1 tsp freshly grated root ginger
1 lemongrass stalk, outer leaves
discarded and finely chopped
2 tbsp lime zest
3–4 tbsp freshly squeezed lime juice
1 tbsp light soy sauce
1 tsp ground cumin
1 tsp ground coriander
$\frac{1}{4}$ tsp ground cinnamon
1.4 kg/3 lb chicken wings (about 12
large wings)
6 tbsp mayonnaise
2 tbsp freshly chopped coriander
lemon or lime wedges, to garnish

Place the low rack in the halogen oven and set the oven to 190°C/375°F. Blend the honey, chilli sauce, garlic, ginger, lemongrass, 1 tablespoon of the lime zest and 2 tablespoons of the lime juice with the soy sauce, cumin, coriander and cinnamon. Bring to the boil and reduce the heat. Simmer for 3 minutes. Stir and leave to cool.

Prepare the chicken wings by folding the tips back under the thickest part of the meat to form a triangle. Arrange in an ovenproof dish. Pour over the honey mixture, turning the wings to ensure that they are all well coated. Cover with clingfilm and leave to marinate in the refrigerator for 4 hours, or overnight, turning once or twice.

Mix together the mayonnaise with the remaining lime zest and juice and the coriander. Leave to allow the flavours to develop while the wings are cooking.

Set the oven to 185°C/365°F. Arrange the wings on the high rack, which should be covered with kitchen foil, and place in the oven. Roast for 30–35 minutes until the wings are tender and golden, basting once or twice with the remaining marinade and turning once. Watch the wings carefully towards the end of cooking to make sure they do not burn. Remove from the oven. Garnish the wings with lemon or lime wedges and serve immediately with the mayonnaise.

Chicken Baked in a Salt Crust

Serves 4

1.4 kg/3 lb oven-ready chicken
salt and freshly ground black pepper
1 medium onion, peeled
fresh rosemary sprig
fresh thyme sprig
1 bay leaf
15 g/¹/₂ oz butter, softened
1 garlic clove, peeled and crushed
pinch of ground paprika
finely grated zest of ¹/₂ lemon

For the salt crust:

900 g/2 lb plain flour
450 g/1 lb fine cooking salt
450 g/1 lb coarse sea salt
2 tbsp oil

To garnish:

fresh herbs
lemon slices

Fit the extender to the halogen oven bowl and place the low rack in the oven. Set the oven to 180°C/350°F. Remove the giblets if necessary and rinse the chicken with cold water. Sprinkle the inside with salt and pepper. Put the onion inside with the rosemary, thyme and bay leaf.

Mix the butter, garlic, paprika and lemon zest together. Starting at the neck end, gently ease the skin from the chicken and push the mixture under.

To make the salt crust, put the flour and salts in a large mixing bowl and stir together. Make a well in the centre. Pour in 600 ml/1 pint cold water and the oil. Mix to a stiff dough, then knead on a lightly floured surface for 2–3 minutes. Roll out to a circle with a diameter of about 51 cm/20 inches. Place the chicken breast-side down in the middle. Lightly brush the edges with water, then fold over to enclose. Pinch the joins together to seal.

Put the chicken join-side down in a roasting tin that will fit, or use an ovenproof tray. Place in the oven. Switch the timer to 1 hour and close the lid. Check the chicken is still intact in the salt crust and continue to cook for a further 1¹/₂ hours. Remove from the oven and stand for 20 minutes.

Break open the hard crust and remove the chicken. Discard the crust. Remove the skin from the chicken, garnish with the fresh herbs and lemon slices. Serve the chicken immediately.

Herb-baked Chicken with Tagliatelle

Serves 4

75 g/3 oz fresh white breadcrumbs
3 tbsp olive oil
1 tsp dried oregano
2 tbsp sun-dried tomato purée
salt and freshly ground black pepper
4 skinless, boneless chicken breasts,
each about 150 g/5 oz
2 x 400 g cans plum tomatoes
4 tbsp freshly shredded basil
2 tbsp dry white wine
350 g/12 oz tagliatelle
fresh basil sprigs, to garnish

Fit the extender to the halogen oven bowl and place the low rack in the oven. Set the oven to 190°C/375°F. Mix together the breadcrumbs, 1 tablespoon of the olive oil, the oregano and tomato purée. Season to taste with salt and pepper. Place the chicken breasts in a roasting tin or on an ovenproof tray. Coat with the breadcrumb mixture.

Mix the plum tomatoes with the shredded basil and white wine. Season to taste, then spoon evenly round the chicken.

Drizzle the remaining olive oil over the chicken breasts and cook in the oven for 20 minutes, or until the chicken is golden and the juices run clear when a skewer is inserted into the flesh.

Meanwhile, bring a large pan of lightly salted water to a rolling boil. Add the pasta and cook according to the packet instructions, or until *al dente*.

Drain the pasta thoroughly and transfer to warmed serving plates. Arrange the chicken breasts on top of the pasta and spoon over the sauce. Garnish with sprigs of basil and serve immediately.

Sticky-glazed Spatchcocked Poussins

Serves 4

2 poussins, each about 700 g/1½lb
salt and freshly ground
black pepper
4 kumquats, thinly sliced (optional),
or use mandarin segments
assorted salad leaves, crusty bread
or new potatoes, to serve

For the glaze:

zest of 1 small lemon, finely grated
1 tbsp lemon juice
1 tbsp dry sherry
2 tbsp clear honey
2 tbsp dark soy sauce
2 tbsp wholegrain mustard
1 tsp tomato purée
½ tsp Chinese five-spice powder

Fit the extender to the oven bowl and place both the racks in the oven. Set the oven to 180°C/350°F. Place one of the poussins breast-side down on a board. Using poultry shears, cut down one side of the backbone. Cut down the other side of the backbone. Remove the bone. Open out the poussin and press down hard on the breast bone with the heel of your hand to break it and to flatten the poussin. Push two skewers crossways through the bird to keep it flat, ensuring that each skewer goes through a wing and out through the leg on the opposite side. Repeat with the other bird. Season both sides of the bird with salt and pepper.

To make the glaze, mix together the lemon zest and juice, sherry, honey, soy sauce, mustard, tomato purée and Chinese five-spice powder and use to brush all over the poussins.

Place one poussin skin-side down on each of the racks, or use a foil-lined tray. Close the lid, switch the timer on and cook for 15 minutes, brushing halfway through with more glaze. Turn and swap the poussins over. Continue to cook for 10 minutes. If not cooked, brush again with glaze and cook for a further 10–15 minutes, until well browned and cooked through. If they start to brown too quickly, turn the temperature down a little. Arrange the kumquat or mandarin on top and brush with a little glaze. Remove the skewers and cut each poussin in half along the breastbone. Serve immediately with the salad and crusty bread or new potatoes.

Crispy Duck Legs with Pancakes

Serves 6

900 g/2 lb plums, halved
25 g/1 oz butter
2 star anise
1 tsp freshly grated root ginger
50 g/2 oz soft brown sugar
zest and juice of 1 orange
freshly ground black pepper
4 duck legs
3 tbsp dark soy sauce
2 tbsp dark brown sugar
$^1/_2$ tsp salt
$^1/_2$ cucumber, cut into matchsticks
1 small bunch spring onions, trimmed and shredded
18 ready-made Chinese pancakes, warmed

Fit the extender to the halogen oven bowl and place the high rack inside. Set the oven to 200˚C/400˚F. Stone the plums and place in a saucepan with the butter, star anise, ginger, brown sugar and orange zest and juice. Season to taste with pepper. Cook over a gentle heat until the sugar has dissolved. Bring to the boil, then reduce heat and simmer for 10–15 minutes, stirring occasionally, until the plums are soft and the mixture is thick. Remove the star anise. Leave to cool.

Using a fork, prick the duck legs all over. Place in a large bowl and pour boiling water over to remove some of the fat. Drain, pat dry on absorbent kitchen paper and leave until cold.

Mix together the soy sauce, dark brown sugar and the $^1/_2$ teaspoon salt. Rub this mixture generously over the duck legs. Place the duck legs on the high rack and place an ovenproof tray underneath. Roast in the oven for 30–40 minutes, or until well cooked and the skin is browned and crisp. Remove from the oven and leave to rest for 10 minutes.

Shred the duck meat, using a fork to hold the hot duck leg and another to remove the meat. Transfer to a warmed serving platter with the cucumber and spring onions. Serve immediately with the plum compote and warmed pancakes.

Chilli Roast Chicken

Serves 4

3 medium-hot, fresh red
chillies, deseeded
$1/2$ tsp ground turmeric
1 tsp cumin seeds
1 tsp coriander seeds
2 garlic cloves, peeled and crushed
2.5 cm/1 inch piece fresh root ginger,
peeled and chopped
1 tbsp lemon juice
1 tbsp olive oil
2 tbsp roughly chopped fresh
coriander
$1/2$ tsp salt
freshly ground black pepper
1.4 kg/3 lb oven-ready chicken
15 g/$1/2$ oz unsalted butter, melted
450 g/1 lb butternut squash
fresh parsley and coriander sprigs,
to garnish

To serve:

4 baked potatoes
seasonal green vegetables

Fit the extender to the halogen oven bowl and place both racks in the bowl. Set the oven to 190°C/375°F. Roughly chop the chillies and put in a food processor with the turmeric, cumin seeds, coriander seeds, garlic, ginger, lemon juice, olive oil, coriander, salt, pepper and 2 tablespoons of cold water. Blend to a paste, leaving the ingredients still slightly chunky.

Starting at the neck end of the chicken, gently ease up the skin to loosen it from the breast. Reserve 3 tablespoons of the paste. Push the remaining paste over the chicken breast under the skin, spreading it evenly.

Put the chicken in a roasting tin that will fit in the oven, or use an ovenproof tray. Mix the reserved chilli paste with the melted butter. Brush 1 tablespoon evenly over the chicken then place the chicken on the high rack and roast for 20 minutes.

Meanwhile, halve, peel and scoop out the seeds from the butternut squash. Cut into chunks and mix in the remaining chilli paste and butter mixture. Place the butternut squash on an ovenproof tray and place on the low rack. Continue to roast for a further 1 hour, occasionally basting with the cooking juices, until the chicken is fully cooked and the squash is tender. Garnish with parsley and coriander. Serve hot with baked potatoes and green vegetables.

Chicken Parcels with Courgettes

Serves 4

2 tbsp olive oil
125 g/4 oz farfalle pasta
1 onion, peeled and thinly sliced
1 garlic clove, peeled and
finely chopped
2 medium courgettes, trimmed and
thinly sliced
salt and freshly ground
black pepper
2 tbsp freshly chopped oregano
4 plum tomatoes, deseeded and
coarsely chopped
4 x 175 g/6 oz skinless, boneless
chicken breasts
150 ml/¼ pint Italian white wine

Fit the extender to the halogen oven bowl and place the high rack in the oven. Set the oven to 190°C/375°F. Lightly brush four large sheets of nonstick baking parchment with half the oil. Bring a saucepan of lightly salted water to the boil and cook the pasta for 10 minutes, or until *al dente*. Drain and reserve.

Pour the remaining oil into a medium-sized saucepan, add the onion and garlic and cook for 3 minutes. Add the courgettes and cook for 1 minute, then remove from the heat, season to taste with salt and pepper and add half the oregano.

Divide the cooked pasta equally between the four sheets of baking parchment, positioning the pasta in the centre. Top the pasta with equal amounts of the vegetable mixture, and sprinkle a quarter of the chopped tomatoes over each.

Score the surface of each chicken breast about 1 cm/½ inch deep. Place a chicken breast on top of the pasta and sprinkle each with the remaining oregano and the white wine. Fold the edges of the paper along the top, then along each side, creating a sealed envelope.

Arrange the parcels on the rack. Bake in the oven for 30–35 minutes until cooked. Serve immediately.

Pheasant with Sage Blueberries

Serves 4

3 tbsp olive oil
3 shallots, peeled and
roughly chopped
2 fresh sage sprigs,
roughly chopped
1 bay leaf
1 lemon, halved
salt and freshly ground
black pepper
2 pheasants or guinea fowl, rinsed
and dried
125 g/4 oz blueberries
4 slices Parma ham or bacon
125 ml/4 fl oz vermouth or dry
white wine
200 ml/^{1}/$_3$ pint chicken stock
3 tbsp double cream or
butter (optional)
1 tbsp brandy
roast potatoes, to serve

Fit the extender to the halogen oven bowl and place the low rack inside. Set the oven to 180°C/350°F. Place the oil, shallots, sage and bay leaf in a bowl with the juice from the lemon halves. Season with salt and pepper. Tuck each of the squeezed lemon halves into the birds with 75 g/3 oz of the blueberries, then rub the birds with the marinade and leave for 2–3 hours, basting occasionally.

Remove the birds from the marinade and cover each with 2 slices of Parma ham. Tie the legs of each bird with string and place in a roasting tin, or an ovenproof tray. Pour over the marinade and add the vermouth or wine. Roast in the oven for 1 hour, or until tender and golden and the juices run clear when a thigh is pierced with a sharp knife or skewer. Transfer to a warm serving plate, cover with kitchen foil and discard the string. Skim off any surface fat from the tin and set over a medium-high heat.

Add the stock to the tin and bring to the boil, scraping any browned bits from the bottom. Boil until slightly reduced. Whisk in the cream or butter, if using, and simmer until thickened, whisking constantly. Stir in the brandy and strain into a gravy jug. Add the remaining blueberries and keep warm.

Using a sharp carving knife, cut each of the birds in half and arrange on the plate with the crispy Parma ham. Serve immediately with roast potatoes and the gravy.

Saffron Chicken with Crispy Onions

Serves 4

1.4 kg/3 lb oven-ready chicken,
preferably free range
50 g/2 oz butter, softened
1 tsp saffron strands, lightly toasted
grated zest of 1 lemon
2 tbsp freshly chopped
flat-leaf parsley
2 tbsp extra virgin olive oil
450 g/1 lb onions, peeled and cut
into thin wedges
8–12 garlic cloves, peeled
1 tsp cumin seeds
$^{1}/_{2}$ tsp ground cinnamon
50 g/2 oz pine nuts
50 g/2 oz sultanas
salt and freshly ground black pepper
fresh flat-leaf parsley sprig,
to garnish

Fit the extender to the halogen oven bowl and place the low rack inside. Set the oven to 190°C/375°F. Using your fingertips, gently loosen the skin from the chicken breast by sliding your hand between the skin and flesh. Cream together 50 g/2 oz of the butter with the saffron strands, the lemon zest and half the parsley, until smooth. Push the butter under the skin. Spread over the breast and the top of the thighs with your fingers. Pull the neck skin to tighten the skin over the breast and tuck under the bird, then secure with a skewer or cocktail stick.

Heat the olive oil and remaining butter in a frying pan and cook the onions and garlic cloves for 5–8 minutes until the onions are soft. Stir in the cumin seeds, cinnamon, pine nuts and sultanas and cook for 2 minutes. Season to taste with salt and pepper and place in a roasting tin that fits, or an ovenproof tray.

Place the chicken, breast-side down, on the onions and place in the oven. Roast for 45 minutes. Reduce the oven temperature to 175°C/350°F. Turn the chicken breast-side up and stir the onions. Continue to roast for 30–35 minutes until the chicken is a deep golden yellow and the onions are crisp. Allow to rest for 10 minutes, then sprinkle with the remaining parsley. Before serving, garnish with a sprig of parsley and serve immediately with the onions and garlic.

Pheasant with Red Wine Gravy

Serves 4

25 g/1 oz butter

1 tbsp olive oil

2 small pheasants (preferably hens) rinsed, well dried and halved

8 shallots, peeled

300 g/11 oz portabello mushrooms, thickly sliced

2–3 fresh thyme or rosemary sprigs, leaves stripped

300 ml/¹/₂ pint Valpolicella or fruity red wine

300 ml/¹/₂ pint chicken stock, heated

1 tbsp cornflour

2 tbsp balsamic vinegar

2 tbsp redcurrant jelly, or to taste

2 tbsp freshly chopped flat-leaf parsley

salt and freshly ground black pepper

fresh thyme sprigs, to garnish

Fit the extender to the halogen oven bowl and place the low rack inside. Set the oven to 180°C/350°F. Heat the butter and oil in a frying pan. Add the pheasant halves and shallots, working in batches if necessary, and cook for 10 minutes, or until golden on all sides, shaking the pan to glaze the shallots. Transfer to a casserole dish or roasting tin that fits in the oven. Add the mushrooms and thyme to the fat left in the pan. Cook for 2–3 minutes until beginning to colour. Add to the pheasants.

Add the wine to the saucepan – it will bubble and steam. Cook, stirring up any browned bits from the bottom of the pan and allow to reduce by half. Pour in the stock and bring to the boil, then pour over the pheasant halves. Cover and place in the oven and cook for 50 minutes, or until tender. Remove the pheasant halves and vegetables to a wide, shallow serving dish and set the casserole dish or roasting tin over a medium-high heat.

Skim off any surface fat and bring to the boil. Blend the cornflour with the vinegar and stir into the sauce with the redcurrant jelly. Boil until the sauce is reduced and thickened slightly. Stir in the parsley and season to taste with salt and pepper. Pour over the pheasant halves, garnish with sprigs of fresh thyme and serve immediately.

Sweet Potato Chicken Pie

Serves 4

700 g/1¹/₂ lb sweet potatoes, peeled
and cut into chunks
150 ml/¹/₄ pint milk
25 g/1 oz butter
2 tsp brown sugar
grated zest of 1 orange
salt and freshly ground black pepper
4 skinless chicken breast
fillets, diced
1 medium onion, peeled and
roughly chopped
125 g/4 oz baby mushrooms,
stems trimmed
2 leeks, trimmed and thickly sliced
150 ml/¹/₄ pint dry white wine
1 chicken stock cube
1 tbsp freshly chopped parsley
50 ml/2 fl oz crème fraîche or thick
double cream
green vegetables, to serve

Fit the extender to the halogen oven bowl and place the low rack inside. Set the oven to 180˚C/350˚F. Cook the potatoes in lightly salted, boiling water until tender. Drain well, then return to the saucepan and mash until smooth and creamy, gradually adding the milk, then the butter, sugar and orange zest. Season to taste with salt and pepper and reserve.

Place the chicken in an ovenproof dish with the onion, mushrooms, leeks, wine and stock cube and season to taste. Place in the oven, close the lid and cook for 20 minutes, or until the chicken and vegetables are tender. Remove the chicken mixture from the oven and allow to cool for 5 minutes.

Using a slotted spoon, transfer the chicken and vegetables to a 1.1litre/2 pint pie dish, checking the dish fits in the oven. Add the parsley and crème fraîche or cream to the liquid in the pan and pour into a saucepan. Bring to the boil. Simmer until thickened and smooth, stirring constantly. Pour over the chicken in the pie dish, mix and cool.

Spread the mashed potato over the chicken filling, and swirl the surface into decorative peaks. Return to the oven, placing the dish on the low rack. Close the lid and cook for 20–25 minutes until the top is golden. Serve immediately with fresh green vegetables.

Lemon Chicken with Rosemary

Serves 6

12 skinless, boneless chicken thighs
1 large lemon
125 ml/4 fl oz extra virgin olive oil
6 garlic cloves, peeled and sliced
2 onions, peeled and thinly sliced
bunch fresh rosemary
1.1 kg/2^1/$_2$ lb potatoes, peeled and
cut into 4 cm/1^1/$_2$ inch pieces
salt and freshly ground black pepper
18–24 black olives, pitted

To serve:

steamed carrots
courgettes

Fit the extender to the halogen oven bowl and place the low rack inside. Set the oven to 190˚C/375˚F. Trim the chicken thighs and place in a deep, ovenproof dish. Remove the zest from the lemon with a zester or, if using a peeler, cut into thin julienne strips. Reserve half and add the remainder to the chicken. Squeeze the lemon juice over the chicken, toss to coat well and leave to stand for 10 minutes.

Add the remaining lemon zest or julienne strips, olive oil, garlic, onions and half of the rosemary sprigs. Toss gently and leave for about 20 minutes.

Cover the potatoes in lightly salted water and bring to the boil. Cook for 2 minutes, then drain well and add to the chicken. Season to taste with salt and pepper.

Roast the chicken in the oven for 45–50 minutes until cooked, turning the chicken and potatoes over 1–2 times. When cooked, discard the rosemary, and add fresh sprigs of rosemary. Add the olives and stir. Serve immediately with steamed carrots and courgettes.

Turkey Tetrazzini

Serves 4

275 g/10 oz green and white
tagliatelle
50 g/2 oz butter
4 slices streaky bacon, diced
1 onion, peeled and finely chopped
175 g/6 oz mushrooms, thinly sliced
40 g/1¹/₂ oz plain flour
450 ml/³/₄ pint chicken stock
150 ml/¹/₄ pint double cream
2 tbsp sherry
450 g/1 lb cooked turkey meat, cut
into bite-size pieces
1 tbsp freshly chopped parsley
freshly grated nutmeg
salt and freshly ground black pepper
25 g/1 oz Parmesan cheese, grated

Fit the extender to the halogen oven bowl and place the low rack inside. Set the oven to 180˚C/350˚F. Lightly oil a large, ovenproof dish. Bring a large saucepan of lightly salted water to the boil. Add the tagliatelle and cook for 7–9 minutes until *al dente*. Drain well and reserve.

In a medium-size saucepan, heat the butter and add the bacon. Cook for 2–3 minutes until crisp and golden. Add the onion and mushrooms and cook for 3–4 minutes until the vegetables are tender.

Stir in the flour and cook for 2 minutes. Remove from the heat and slowly stir in the stock. Return to the heat and cook, stirring, until a smooth, thick sauce has formed. Add the tagliatelle, and then pour in the cream and sherry. Add the turkey and parsley. Season to taste with the nutmeg and salt and pepper. Toss well to coat.

Turn the mixture into the prepared dish, spreading evenly. Sprinkle the top with the Parmesan cheese. Place on the rack in the oven. Bake for 30–35 minutes until crisp, golden and bubbling. Garnish with chopped parsley and Parmesan cheese. Serve straight from the dish.

Orange Roasted Whole Chicken

Serves 4

1 small orange, thinly sliced
50 g/2 oz sugar
1.4 kg/3 lb oven-ready chicken
1 small bunch fresh coriander
1 small bunch fresh mint
2 tbsp olive oil
1 tsp Chinese five-spice powder
1/2 tsp paprika
1 tsp fennel seeds, crushed
salt and freshly ground black pepper
fresh coriander sprigs,
to garnish
freshly cooked vegetables, to serve

Fit the extender to the halogen oven bowl and place the low rack inside. Set the oven to 190˚C/375˚F. Place the orange slices in a small saucepan, cover with water, bring to the boil, then simmer for 2 minutes and drain. Place the sugar in a clean saucepan with 150 ml/1/4 pint fresh water. Stir over a low heat until the sugar dissolves, then bring to the boil, add the drained orange slices and simmer for 10 minutes. Remove from the heat and leave in the syrup until cold.

Remove any excess fat from inside the chicken. Starting at the neck end, carefully loosen the skin of the chicken over the breast and legs without tearing. Push the orange slices under the loosened skin with the coriander and mint.

Mix together the olive oil, Chinese five-spice powder, paprika and crushed fennel seeds and season to taste with salt and pepper. Brush the chicken skin generously with this mixture. Place the chicken on an ovenproof tray or in a roasting tin and place on the rack. Roast in the oven for 1–1 1/2 hours until the juices run clear when a skewer is inserted into the thickest part of the thigh. Remove from the oven and leave to rest for 10 minutes. Garnish with sprigs of fresh coriander and serve with freshly cooked vegetables.

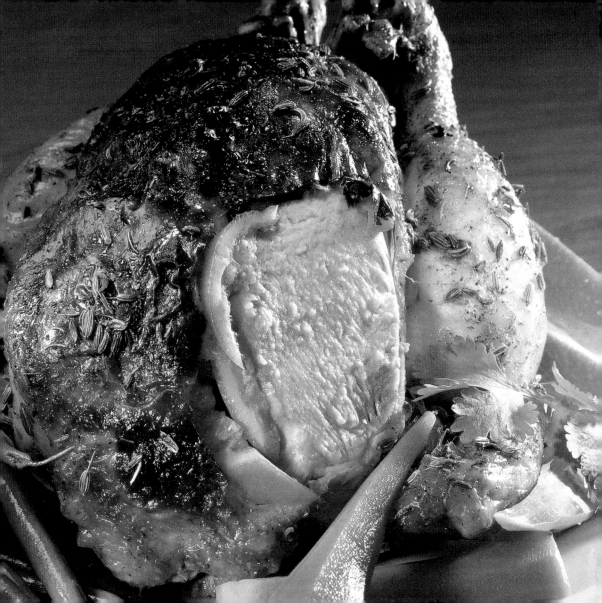

Pasta Pepper Salad

Serves 4

4 tbsp olive oil
1 each red, orange and yellow pepper, deseeded and cut into chunks
1 large courgette, trimmed and cut into chunks
1 medium aubergine, trimmed and diced
275 g/10 oz fusilli
4 plum tomatoes, quartered
1 bunch fresh basil leaves, roughly chopped
2 tbsp pesto
2 garlic cloves, peeled and roughly chopped
1 tbsp lemon juice
225 g/8 oz skinless, boneless roasted chicken breast
salt and freshly ground black pepper
125 g/4 oz feta cheese, crumbled
crusty bread, to serve

Fit the extender to the halogen oven bowl and place the low rack inside. Set the oven to 190°C/375°F. Spoon the olive oil into a deep roasting tin and heat on the hob for 2 minutes, or until very hot. Add the peppers, courgette and aubergine and stir until coated. Place in the oven and roast for 30 minutes, or until beginning to char, stirring occasionally.

Meanwhile, bring a large pan of lightly salted water to a rolling boil. Add the pasta and cook according to the packet instructions, or until *al dente*. Drain and refresh under cold running water. Drain thoroughly, place in a large salad bowl and reserve.

Remove the cooked vegetables from the oven and allow to cool. Add to the cooled pasta, together with the quartered tomatoes, chopped basil leaves, pesto, garlic and lemon juice. Toss lightly to mix.

Shred the chicken roughly into small pieces and stir into the pasta and vegetable mixture. Season to taste with salt and pepper, then sprinkle the crumbled feta cheese over the pasta and stir gently. Cover the dish and leave to marinate for 30 minutes, stirring occasionally. Serve the salad with fresh crusty bread.

Chicken Mushroom Filo Pie

Serves 4

1 onion, peeled and chopped
1 leek, trimmed and chopped
225 ml/8 fl oz chicken stock
3 x 175 g/6 oz chicken breasts
150 ml/¼ pint dry white wine
1 bay leaf
175 g/6 oz baby button mushrooms
2 tbsp plain flour
1 tbsp freshly chopped tarragon
salt and freshly ground black pepper
fresh parsley sprig, to garnish
seasonal vegetables, to serve

For the topping:

75 g/3 oz (about 5 sheets) filo pastry
1 tbsp sunflower oil
1 tsp sesame seeds

Fit the extender to the halogen oven bowl and place the low rack inside. Set the oven to 190°C/375°F. Put the onion and leek into a medium saucepan. Pour in 125 ml/4 fl oz of the stock and cover with a lid.

Bring to the boil, then lower the heat to a simmer. Cook for 5–10 minutes until all the stock has evaporated and the vegetables are tender.

Cut the chicken into bite-size cubes. Add to the vegetables with the remaining stock, wine, bay leaf and mushrooms. Cover with the lid and return to the hob. Bring to the boil, then reduce the heat and simmer for 10 minutes.

Blend the flour with 3 tablespoons cold water. Stir into the vegetables and stir until well incorporated. Add the tarragon with seasoning. Spoon the mixture into a 1.2 litre/2 pint pie dish that fits, discarding the bay leaf.

Lightly brush a sheet of filo pastry with a little of the oil. Crumple the pastry slightly. Arrange on top of the filling. Repeat with the remaining filo sheets and oil, then sprinkle the top of the pie with the sesame seeds.

Place on the low rack and bake for 20 minutes, or until the filo pastry topping is golden and crisp. Garnish with a sprig of parsley. Serve the pie immediately with the seasonal vegetables.

Chinese Barbecue-style Quails

Serves 4

4 quails
2 tbsp salt
3 tbsp hoisin sauce
1 tbsp Chinese rice wine or
dry sherry
1 tbsp light soy sauce
700 g/1¹/₂ lb aubergines, trimmed
and cubed
1 tbsp oil
4 garlic cloves, peeled and
finely chopped
1 tbsp freshly chopped root ginger
6 spring onions, trimmed and
finely chopped
3 tbsp dark soy sauce
¹/₄ tsp dried chilli flakes
1 tbsp yellow bean sauce
1 tbsp sugar

To garnish:

sliced red chilli
fresh coriander sprigs

Fit the extender to the halogen oven bowl and place the low rack inside. Set the oven to 200°C/400°F. Rub the quails inside and out with 1 tablespoon of the salt. Mix together the hoisin sauce, Chinese rice wine or sherry and light soy sauce. Rub the quails inside and out with the sauce. Place in a small roasting tin or ovenproof dish and roast in the oven for 10 minutes. Reduce the heat to 180°C/350°F and continue to roast for 20 minutes, or until tender. Remove the quails and leave to rest for 10 minutes.

Place the aubergines in a colander and sprinkle with the remaining salt. Leave to drain for 20 minutes, then rinse under cold running water and pat dry with absorbent kitchen paper. Heat a wok or large frying pan over a moderate heat. Add the oil and, when hot, add the aubergines, garlic, ginger and 4 of the spring onions and cook for 1 minute. Add the dark soy sauce, chilli flakes, yellow bean sauce, sugar and 450 ml/³/₄ pint water. Bring to the boil, then simmer uncovered for 10–15 minutes.

Increase the heat to high and continue to cook, stirring occasionally, until the sauce is reduced and slightly thickened. Spoon the aubergine mixture onto warmed individual plates and top with a quail. Garnish with the remaining spring onion, fresh chilli and a sprig of coriander and serve immediately.

Chicken Tikka Masala

Serves 4

4 skinless chicken breast fillets
150 ml/¹/₄ pint natural yogurt
1 garlic clove, peeled and crushed
2.5 cm/1 inch piece fresh root ginger,
peeled and grated
1 tsp chilli powder
1 tbsp ground coriander
2 tbsp lime juice
lime twist, to garnish
freshly cooked rice, to serve

For the masala sauce:

15 g/1/2 oz unsalted butter
2 tbsp sunflower oil
1 onion, peeled and chopped
1 green chilli, deseeded and finely
chopped
1 tsp garam masala
150 ml/¹/₄ pint double cream
salt and freshly ground black pepper
3 tbsp fresh coriander leaves,
roughly torn

Place the low rack inside the halogen oven and set the oven to 200°C/400°F. Cut each chicken breast across into three pieces, and then make two or three shallow cuts in each piece. Put in a shallow dish. Mix together the yogurt, garlic, ginger, chilli powder, ground coriander and lime juice. Pour over the chicken, cover and marinate in the refrigerator for up to 24 hours.

Remove the chicken from the marinade and arrange on an oiled ovenproof tray that will fit in the oven. Bake in the oven for 15 minutes, or until golden brown and cooked.

While the chicken is cooking, heat the butter and oil in a wok or frying pan and fry the onion for 5 minutes, or until tender. Add the chilli and garam masala and fry for a few more seconds. Stir in the cream and remaining marinade. Simmer over a low heat for 1 minute, stirring all the time.

Add the chicken pieces and cook for a further 1 minute, stirring to coat in the sauce. Season to taste with salt and pepper. Transfer the chicken pieces to a warmed serving plate. Stir the chopped coriander into the sauce, then spoon over the chicken, garnish and serve immediately with freshly cooked rice.

Fish & Seafood

Whether it's roasting, grilling or baking, with a halogen oven there are plenty of routes to a perfect fish dish. This chapter provides you with a selection of flavoursome options ranging from zesty to creamy, from spicy to cheesy. For a cold winter's day, try the hearty Traditional Fish Pie, whilst the Parmesan & Garlic Lobster is the perfect choice for a special occasion. For those who prefer a pasta- or potato-based dish there's Tuna Cannelloni or Supreme Baked Potatoes.

Traditional Fish Pie

Serves 4

450 g/1 lb cod or coley
fillets, skinned
450 ml/³/₄ pint milk
1 small onion, peeled
and quartered
salt and freshly ground
black pepper
900 g/2 lb potatoes, peeled and
cut into chunks
100 g/3¹/₂ oz butter
125 g/4 oz large prawns, peeled
2 large eggs, hard-boiled
and quartered
198 g can sweetcorn, drained
2 tbsp freshly chopped parsley
3 tbsp plain flour
50 g/2 oz Cheddar cheese, grated

Place the low rack in the halogen oven and set the oven to 175°C/350°F. Put the fish in a dish. Pour over 300 ml/¹/₂ pint of the milk and add the onion. Season to taste with salt and pepper. Cook in the oven for 8–10 minutes until the fish is cooked. Leave until cool enough to handle, then remove the dish from the oven.

Spoon the fish into a deep, 1.4 litre/2¹/₂ pint, ovenproof dish. Strain the cooking liquid and reserve.

Boil the potatoes until soft, then mash with 40 g/1¹/₂ oz of the butter and 2–3 tablespoons of the remaining milk. Reserve.

Arrange the prawns and sliced eggs on top of the fish, then scatter over the sweetcorn and sprinkle with the parsley.

Melt the remaining butter in a saucepan, stir in the flour and cook gently for 1 minute, stirring. Whisk in the reserved cooking liquid and remaining milk. Cook for 2 minutes, or until thickened, then pour over the fish mixture and cool slightly.

Spread the mashed potato over the top of the pie and sprinkle over the grated cheese. Switch the oven to 190°C/375°F. Bake in the oven for 25–30 minutes until golden. Serve immediately.

Fish Lasagne

Serves 4

75 g/3 oz mushrooms
1 tsp sunflower oil
1 small onion, peeled and
finely chopped
1 tbsp freshly chopped oregano
400 g can chopped tomatoes
1 tbsp tomato purée
salt and freshly ground black pepper
450 g/1 lb cod or haddock
fillets, skinned
9–12 sheets precooked
lasagne verde
mixed salad leaves and cherry
tomatoes, to serve

For the topping:
1 medium egg, beaten
125 g/4 oz cottage cheese
150 ml/¹/₄ pint natural yogurt
50 g/2 oz half-fat Cheddar
cheese, grated

Place the low rack in the halogen oven and set the oven to 190°C/375°F. Wipe the mushrooms, trim the stalks and chop. Heat the oil in a large, heavy-based pan, add the onion and gently cook the onion for 3–5 minutes until soft.

Stir in the mushrooms, the oregano and the chopped tomatoes with their juice. Blend the tomato purée with 1 tablespoon water. Stir into the pan and season to taste with salt and pepper. Bring the sauce to the boil, then simmer uncovered for 5–10 minutes.

Remove as many of the tiny pin bones as possible from the fish and cut into cubes and add to the tomato sauce mixture. Stir gently and remove the pan from the heat.

Cover the base of an ovenproof gratin dish (check it fits in the oven) with 2–3 sheets of the lasagne verde. Top with half of the fish mixture. Repeat the layers, finishing with the lasagne sheets.

To make the topping, mix together the beaten egg, cottage cheese and yogurt. Pour over the lasagne and sprinkle with the cheese. Cook the lasagne in the oven for 30–35 minutes until the topping is golden brown and bubbling. Serve the lasagne immediately with the mixed salad leaves and cherry tomatoes.

Smoked Haddock Tart

Serves 6

For the shortcrust pastry:

150 g/5 oz plain flour

pinch salt

25 g/1 oz lard or white vegetable fat,
cut into small cubes

40 g/1$^{1}/_{2}$ oz butter or hard margarine,
cut into small cubes

For the filling:

225 g/8 oz smoked haddock,
skinned and cubed

2 large eggs, beaten

300 ml/$^{1}/_{2}$ pint double cream

1 tsp Dijon mustard

freshly ground black pepper

125 g/4 oz Gruyère cheese, grated

1 tbsp freshly snipped chives

To serve:

lemon wedges

tomato wedges

fresh green salad leaves

Place the low rack in the halogen oven and set the oven to 200°C/400°F. Sift the flour and salt into a large bowl. Add the fats and mix lightly. Using the fingertips, rub into the flour until the mixture resembles breadcrumbs.

Sprinkle 1 tablespoon of cold water into the mixture and, with a knife, start bringing the dough together. (It may be necessary to use the hands for the final stage.) If the dough does not form a ball instantly, add a little more water. Put the pastry in a polythene bag and chill for at least 30 minutes.

On a lightly floured surface, roll out the pastry and use to line an 18 cm/ 7 inch, lightly oiled quiche or flan tin. Place a piece of kitchen foil or baking parchment in the base and top with baking beans. Bake blind in the oven for 10-12 minutes. Carefully remove the pastry case from the oven and discard the baking beans and kitchen foil. Brush with a little of the beaten egg. Cook for a further 5 minutes, then remove from the oven. Place the fish in the pastry case. Switch the oven to 180°C/350°F.

For the filling, beat together the eggs and cream. Add the mustard, pepper and cheese and pour over the fish. Sprinkle with the chives and bake for 25–30 minutes until the filling is golden brown and set in the centre. If browning too quickly, cover the top with kitchen foil. Serve hot or cold with the lemon and tomato wedges and salad leaves.

Grilled Snapper with Roasted Pepper

Serves 4

1 medium red pepper
1 medium green pepper
4–8 snapper fillets, depending on
size, about 450 g/1 lb
sea salt and freshly ground
black pepper
1 tbsp olive oil
5 tbsp double cream
125 ml/4 fl oz white wine
1 tbsp freshly chopped dill
fresh dill sprigs, to garnish
freshly cooked tagliatelle, to serve

Line the high rack with kitchen foil and place in the halogen oven. Set the oven to 200˚C/400˚F.

Cut the tops off the peppers and divide into quarters. Remove the seeds and the membrane, and then place on the foil-lined rack. Cook for 8–10 minutes until the skins are charred. Remove from the rack, place in a polythene bag and leave until cool. When the peppers are cool, peel and slice thinly. Reserve.

Cover the rack with another piece of kitchen foil and place the snapper fillets skin-side up on the rack. Season to taste with salt and pepper and brush with a little of the olive oil. Cook in the oven for 10–12 minutes, turning over once and brushing again with a little olive oil.

Pour the cream and wine into a small saucepan, bring to the boil and simmer for about 5 minutes until the sauce has thickened slightly. Add the dill, season to taste and stir in the sliced peppers.

Arrange the cooked snapper fillets on warmed serving plates and pour over the cream and pepper sauce. Garnish with sprigs of dill and serve immediately with freshly cooked tagliatelle.

Salmon with Herbed Potatoes

Serves 4

450 g/1 lb baby new potatoes
4 salmon steaks, each weighing
about 175 g/6 oz
1 carrot, peeled and cut into
fine strips
175 g/6 oz short asparagus
spears, trimmed
175 g/6 oz sugar snap
peas, trimmed
finely grated zest and juice of
1 lemon
salt and freshly ground black pepper
25 g/1 oz butter
4 large fresh parsley sprigs

Place the low rack in the halogen oven and set the oven to 190˚C/375˚F. Cook the potatoes in lightly salted, boiling water for 12–15 minutes until just tender. Drain and reserve.

Cut out four pieces of baking parchment, measuring 20.5 cm/ 8 inches square, and place on the work surface. Arrange the potatoes on top. Wipe the salmon steaks and place on top of the potatoes.

Bring a pan of lightly salted water to the boil, then add the carrot strips with the asparagus spears and sugar snaps and simmer for 5–8 minutes until just tender. Drain and stir in the lemon zest and juice. Season to taste with salt and pepper. Toss lightly together. Divide the vegetables evenly between the salmon. Dot the top of each parcel with butter and a sprig of parsley.

To wrap a parcel, lift up two opposite sides of the paper and fold the edges together. Twist the paper at the other two ends to seal the parcel well. Repeat with the remaining parcels.

Place the parcels on the rack and cook in the oven for 15 minutes. Place an unopened parcel on each plate and open just before eating.

Gingered Cod Steaks

Serves 4

2.5 cm/1 inch piece root
ginger, peeled
4 spring onions
2 tsp freshly chopped parsley
1 tbsp soft brown sugar
4 x 175 g/6 oz thick cod steaks
salt and freshly ground
black pepper
25 g/1 oz butter
freshly cooked vegetables,
to serve

Line the low rack with kitchen foil and set the halogen oven to 200°C/400°F. Coarsely grate the piece of ginger. Trim the spring onions and cut into thin strips.

Mix the spring onions, ginger, chopped parsley and sugar. Add 1 tablespoon water.

Wipe the fish steaks. Season to taste with salt and pepper. Place onto four separate 20.5 x 20.5 cm/8 x 8 inch kitchen foil squares.

Carefully spoon the spring onion and ginger mixture over the fish. Cut the butter into small cubes and place over the fish. Loosely fold the foil over the steaks to enclose the fish and to make parcels.

Place on the rack and cook for 10–12 minutes until cooked and the flesh has turned opaque. Place the fish parcels on individual serving plates. Serve immediately with the freshly cooked vegetables.

Thai Fish Cakes

Serves 4

1 red chilli, deseeded
and roughly chopped
4 tbsp roughly chopped
fresh coriander
1 garlic clove, peeled and crushed
2 spring onions, trimmed and
roughly chopped
1 lemongrass, outer leaves
discarded and roughly chopped
75 g/3 oz prawns, thawed if frozen
275 g/10 oz cod fillet, skinned, pin
bones removed and cubed
salt and freshly ground
black pepper
sweet chilli dipping sauce, to serve

Place the high rack in the halogen oven and set the oven to 185°C/365°F. Place the chilli, coriander, garlic, spring onions and lemon grass in a food processor and blend together.

Pat the prawns and cod dry with kitchen paper. Add to the food processor and blend until the mixture is roughly chopped. Season to taste with salt and pepper and blend to mix.

Dampen the hands, and then shape heaped tablespoons of the mixture into 12 little patties.

Place the patties on a lightly oiled baking tray or ovenproof plate. Place on the rack and cook for 10–12 minutes until piping hot and cooked through. Turn the patties over halfway through the cooking time. Serve the fish cakes immediately with the sweet chilli sauce for dipping.

Supreme Baked Potatoes

Serves 4

4 large baking potatoes
40 g/1½ oz butter
1 tbsp sunflower oil
1 carrot, peeled and chopped
2 celery stalks, trimmed and
finely chopped
200 g can white crab meat
2 spring onions, trimmed and
finely chopped
salt and freshly ground
black pepper
50 g/2 oz Cheddar cheese, grated
tomato salad, to serve

Place the low rack in the halogen oven and set the oven to 200°C/400°F. Scrub the potatoes and prick all over with a fork. Place the potatoes on the rack and cook for 50–60 minutes until soft to the touch. Allow to cool a little, then cut in half.

Scoop out the cooked potato and turn into a bowl, leaving a reasonably firm potato shell. Mash the cooked potato flesh, then mix in the butter and mash until the butter has melted.

While the potatoes are cooking, heat the oil in a saucepan and cook the carrot and celery for 2 minutes. Cover the pan tightly and continue to cook for another 5 minutes, or until the vegetables are tender.

Add the cooked vegetables to the bowl of mashed potato and mix well. Fold in the crab meat and the spring onions, and then season to taste with salt and pepper.

Pile the mixture back into the potato shells and press in firmly. Sprinkle the grated cheese over the top. Place on the rack and cook the potato halves for 12–15 minutes until hot, golden and bubbling. Serve immediately with a tomato salad.

Foil-baked Fish

Serves 4

For the tomato sauce:

125 ml/4 fl oz olive oil
4 garlic cloves, peeled and
finely chopped
4 shallots, peeled and
finely chopped
400 g can chopped Italian tomatoes
2 tbsp freshly chopped
flat-leaf parsley
3 tbsp basil leaves
salt and freshly ground black pepper

700 g/1¹/₂ lb red mullet, bass or
haddock fillets
450 g/1 lb live mussels
4 squid
8 large raw prawns
2 tbsp olive oil
3 tbsp dry white wine
3 tbsp freshly chopped basil leaves
lemon wedges, to garnish

Place both racks in the halogen oven and set the oven to 190°C/375°F. Heat the olive oil in a frying pan and gently fry the garlic and shallots for 2 minutes. Stir in the tomatoes and simmer for 10 minutes, breaking the tomatoes down with the wooden spoon. Add the parsley and basil, season to taste with salt and pepper and cook for a further 2 minutes. Reserve and keep warm.

Lightly rinse the fish fillets and discard any bones. Divide the fish into four equal portions, Scrub the mussels thoroughly, removing the beard and any barnacles from the shells. Discard any mussels that are open. Clean the squid and cut into rings. Peel the prawns and remove the thin, black intestinal vein that runs down the back.

Cut four large pieces of kitchen foil and brush with olive oil. Place one fish portion in the centre of each piece of kitchen foil. Close tightly together to form parcels. Place two portions on two small baking trays or ovenproof dishes and bake in the oven for 10 minutes, then remove.

Carefully open up the parcels and add the mussels, squid and prawns. Pour in the wine and spoon over a little of the tomato sauce. Sprinkle with the basil leaves and return to the oven and bake for 5 minutes, or until cooked thoroughly. Discard any unopened mussels, then garnish with lemon wedges and serve with the extra tomato sauce.

Haddock with an Olive Crust

Serves 4

12 pitted black olives,
finely chopped
75 g/3 oz fresh white breadcrumbs
1 tbsp freshly chopped tarragon
1 garlic clove, peeled
and crushed
3 spring onions, trimmed and
finely chopped
1 tbsp olive oil
4 x 175 g/6 oz thick, skinless
haddock fillets

To serve:
freshly cooked carrots
freshly cooked green beans

Place the low rack in the halogen oven and set the oven to 190°C/375°F. Place the black olives in a small bowl with the breadcrumbs and add the chopped tarragon.

Add the garlic to the olives with the chopped spring onions and the olive oil. Mix together.

Wipe the fillets with either a clean, damp cloth or damp kitchen paper, then place on a lightly oiled baking tray.

Place spoonfuls of the olive and breadcrumb mixture on top of each fillet and press the mixture down lightly and evenly over the top of the fish.

Bake the fish in the oven for 20–25 minutes until the fish is cooked thoroughly and the topping is golden brown. Serve immediately with the freshly cooked carrots and beans.

Fish Crumble

Serves 6

450 g/1 lb whiting or halibut fillets
300 ml/^{1}/$_2$ pint milk
salt and freshly ground black pepper
1 tbsp sunflower oil
75 g/3 oz butter or margarine
1 medium onion, peeled and
finely chopped
2 leeks, trimmed and sliced
1 medium carrot, peeled and cut into
small dice
2 medium potatoes, peeled and cut
into small pieces
75 g/3 oz plain flour
300 ml/^{1}/$_2$ pint fish or vegetable stock
2 tbsp whipping cream
1 tsp freshly chopped dill
runner beans, to serve

For the topping:
75 g/3 oz butter or margarine
175 g/6 oz plain flour
75 g/3 oz Parmesan cheese, grated
cayenne pepper, to taste

Fit the extender to the halogen oven bowl and place the low rack in the oven. Set the oven to 190°C/375°F.

Oil a 1.4 litre/2^1/$_2$ pint pie dish. Place the fish in a saucepan with the milk, salt and pepper. Bring to the boil, cover and simmer for 8–10 minutes until the fish is cooked. Remove with a slotted spoon, reserving the cooking liquid. Flake the fish into the prepared dish.

Heat the oil and 1 tablespoon of the butter or margarine in a small frying pan and gently fry the onion, leeks, carrot and potatoes for 1–2 minutes. Cover tightly and cook over a gentle heat for a further 10 minutes until softened. Spoon the vegetables over the fish.

Melt the remaining butter or margarine in a saucepan, add the flour and cook for 1 minute, stirring. Whisk in the reserved cooking liquid and the stock. Cook until thickened, and then stir in the cream. Remove from the heat and stir in the dill. Pour over the fish.

To make the topping, rub the butter or margarine into the flour until it resembles breadcrumbs, and then stir in the cheese and cayenne pepper. Sprinkle over the dish, and bake in the oven for 25–30 minutes until piping hot. Serve with runner beans.

Potato Boulangere with Sea Bass

Serves 2

450 g/1 lb potatoes, peeled and
thinly sliced
1 large onion, peeled and
thinly sliced
salt and freshly ground black pepper
300 ml/¹/₂ pint fish or
vegetable stock
75 g/3 oz butter
350 g/12 oz sea bass fillets
fresh flat-leaf parsley sprigs,
to garnish

Place the low rack in the halogen oven and set the oven to 190˚C/375˚F. Lightly grease a 1.4 litre/2¹/₂ pint baking dish with oil or butter. Layer the potato slices and onions alternately in the prepared dish, seasoning each layer with salt and pepper.

Pour the stock over the top, and then cut 50 g/2 oz of the butter into small pieces and dot over the top layer. Place on the rack and cook in the oven for 50–60 minutes. Do not cover the dish at this stage.

Lightly rinse the sea bass fillets and pat dry on absorbent kitchen paper. Melt the remaining butter and use to brush the fish fillets on both sides.

Remove the partly cooked potato and onion mixture from the oven and place the fish on the top. Cook for 12–15 minutes until cooked. Garnish with sprigs of parsley and serve immediately.

Parmesan ❦ Garlic Lobster

Serves 2

1 large cooked lobster
25 g/1 oz unsalted butter
4 garlic cloves, peeled and crushed
1 tbsp plain flour
300 ml/^{1}/$_2$ pint milk
125 g/4 oz Parmesan cheese, grated
sea salt and freshly ground
black pepper
assorted salad leaves, to serve

Fit the extender to the halogen oven bowl and place the high rack in the oven. Set the oven to 180°C/350°F.

Halve the lobster and crack the claws. Remove the gills, green sac behind the head and the black vein running down the body. Place the lobster halves in a shallow, ovenproof dish, or use a tray.

Melt the butter in a small saucepan and gently cook the garlic for 3 minutes until softened. Add the flour and stir over a medium heat for 1 minute. Draw the saucepan off the heat, then gradually stir in the milk, stirring until the sauce thickens.

Return to the heat and cook for 2 minutes, stirring throughout, until smooth and thickened. Stir in half the cheese and continue to cook for 1 minute, and then season to taste with salt and pepper.

Pour the cheese sauce over the lobster halves and sprinkle with the remaining Parmesan cheese. Place on the rack in the oven and cook for 15–20 minutes until heated through and the cheese sauce is golden brown. Serve with assorted salad leaves.

Roasted Cod with Saffron Aïoli

Serves 4

For the saffron aïoli:
2 garlic cloves, peeled
¼ tsp saffron strands
pinch sea salt
1 medium egg yolk
200 ml/7 fl oz extra virgin olive oil
2 tbsp lemon juice

For the marinade:
2 tbsp olive oil
4 garlic cloves, peeled and
finely chopped
1 red onion, peeled and
finely chopped
1 tbsp freshly chopped rosemary
2 tbsp freshly chopped thyme
4–6 sprigs fresh rosemaryf
1 lemon, sliced
4 x 175 g/6 oz thick cod fillets
with skin
freshly cooked vegetables, to serve

Place the low rack in the halogen oven and set the oven to 180˚C/350˚F.

Crush the garlic, saffron and a pinch of salt in a pestle and mortar to form a paste. Place in a blender with the egg yolk and blend for 30 seconds. With the motor running, slowly add the olive oil in a thin, steady stream until the mayonnaise is smooth and thick. Spoon into a small bowl and stir in the lemon juice. Cover and leave in the refrigerator until required.

Combine the olive oil, garlic, red onion, rosemary and thyme for the marinade and leave to infuse for about 10 minutes.

Place the sprigs of rosemary and slices of lemon in the bottom of a lightly oiled roasting tin or ovenproof tray. Add the cod, skinned-side up. Pour over the prepared marinade and leave to marinate in the refrigerator for 15–20 minutes.

Bake in the oven for 15–20 minutes until the cod is cooked and the flesh flakes easily with a fork. Leave the cod to rest for 1 minute before serving with the saffron aïoli and vegetables.

Roasted Monkfish with Parma Ham

Serves 4

700 g/1½ lb monkfish tail
4 bay leaves
4 slices fontina cheese,
rind removed
8 slices Parma ham
225 g/8 oz angel hair pasta
50 g/2 oz butter
zest and juice of 1 lemon
fresh coriander sprigs, to garnish

To serve:

chargrilled courgettes
chargrilled tomatoes

Place the low rack in the halogen oven and set the oven to 200°C/400°F. Discard any skin from the monkfish tail and cut away and discard the central bone. Cut the fish into four equal portions and lay a bay leaf on each fillet, along with a slice of cheese.

Wrap each fillet with 2 slices of the Parma ham, so that the fish is covered completely. Tuck the ends of the Parma ham in and secure with a cocktail stick.

Lightly oil a baking tray or ovenproof plate and place the fish on the tray. Put on the rack in the oven and cook for 12–15 minutes until just tender.

Bring a large saucepan of lightly salted water to the boil, then slowly add the pasta and cook for 5 minutes until *al dente*, or according to the packet instructions. Drain, reserving 2 tablespoons of the cooking liquor. Return the pasta to the saucepan and add the reserved cooking liquor, butter, lemon zest and juice. Toss until the pasta is well coated and glistening.

Twirl the pasta into small nests on four warmed serving plates and top with the monkfish parcels. Garnish with sprigs of coriander and serve with chargrilled courgettes and tomatoes.

Tuna Cannelloni

Serves 4

1 tbsp olive oil
6 spring onions, trimmed and
finely sliced
1 sweet Mediterranean red pepper,
deseeded and finely chopped
200 g can tuna in brine
250 g tub ricotta cheese
zest and juice of 1 lemon
1 tbsp freshly snipped chives
salt and freshly ground
black pepper
8 precooked cannelloni tubes
1 medium egg, beaten
125 g/4 oz cottage cheese
150 ml/$^1/_4$ pint natural yogurt
pinch freshly grated nutmeg
50 g/2 oz mozzarella cheese, grated
tossed green salad, to serve

Place the low rack in the halogen oven and set the oven to 180°C/350°F. Heat the olive oil in a frying pan and cook the spring onions and pepper until soft. Remove from the pan with a slotted draining spoon and place in a large bowl.

Drain the tuna, and then stir into the spring onion and pepper mixture. Beat the ricotta cheese with the lemon zest and juice and the snipped chives and season to taste with salt and pepper. Beat until soft and blended. Add to the tuna and mix together. If the mixture is still a little stiff, add a little extra lemon juice.

With a teaspoon, carefully spoon the mixture into the cannelloni tubes, then lay the filled tubes in a lightly oiled, shallow, ovenproof dish. Beat the egg, cottage cheese, natural yogurt and nutmeg together and pour over the cannelloni tubes. Sprinkle with the grated mozzarella cheese.

Bake in the oven for 15–20 minutes until the topping is golden brown and bubbling. Serve immediately with a tossed green salad.

Cheesy Vegetable & Prawn Bake

Serves 4

175 g/6 oz long-grain rice
1 garlic clove, peeled and crushed
1 large egg, beaten
3 tbsp freshly shredded basil
4 tbsp Parmesan cheese, grated
salt and freshly ground black pepper
125 g/4 oz baby asparagus
spears, trimmed
150 g/5 oz baby carrots, trimmed
150 g/5 oz fine green
beans, trimmed
150 g/5 oz cherry tomatoes
175 g/6 oz peeled prawns,
thawed if frozen
125 g/4 oz mozzarella cheese,
thinly sliced

Place the high rack in the halogen oven and set the oven to 185˚C/365˚F.

Cook the rice in lightly salted boiling water for 12–15 minutes until tender, then drain.

Stir in the garlic, beaten egg, shredded basil and 2 tablespoons of the Parmesan cheese. Season to taste with salt and pepper. Press this mixture into an oiled, deep, 23 cm/9 inch, ovenproof dish and reserve.

Bring a large saucepan of water to the boil, and then drop in the asparagus, carrots and green beans. Return to the boil and cook for 3–4 minutes. Drain and leave to cool.

Quarter or halve the cherry tomatoes and mix them into the cooled vegetables. Spread the prepared vegetables over the rice and top with the prawns. Season to taste with salt and pepper.

Cover the prawns with the mozzarella slices and sprinkle over the remaining Parmesan cheese. Bake in the oven for 20–25 minutes until piping hot and golden brown in places. Serve immediately.

Vegetable *and* Vegetarian Meals

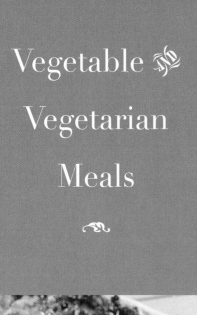

Everyone knows they're good for you, but who says vegetables can't also be the central attraction of a delicious dish? The recipes in this chapter really give vegetables the chance to shine. The Vegetarian Cassoulet is a hearty dish, whilst the Mediterranean flavours of Aubergine & Ravioli Parmigiana or Spinach & Mascarpone Pizza are good enough to transport you to the streets of Italy.

Garlic Herb Roasted Vegetables

Serves 4

1 large garlic bulb
1 onion, peeled and cut into wedges
4 small carrots, peeled and quartered
4 small parsnips, peeled
4 small potatoes, scrubbed and halved
1 fennel bulb, thickly sliced
4 fresh rosemary sprigsf
4 fresh thyme sprigs
2 tbsp olive oil
salt and freshly ground black pepper
200 g/7 oz low-fat soft cheese with herbs and garlic
4 tbsp milk
zest of ¹/₂ lemon
thyme sprigs, to garnish

Fit the extender to the halogen oven bowl and place the low rack inside. Set the oven to 200˚C/400˚F. Cut the garlic in half horizontally. Put into a roasting tin with all the vegetables and herbs.

Add the oil, season well with salt and pepper and toss together to coat lightly in the oil.

Cover with kitchen foil and place on the rack. Roast in the oven for 40 minutes. Remove the kitchen foil and stir. Cook uncovered for 20–30 minutes until all the vegetables are tender and slightly charred. Remove from the oven and allow to cool.

In a small saucepan, melt the low-fat soft cheese together with the milk and lemon zest.

Remove the garlic from the roasting tin and squeeze the flesh into a bowl. Mash thoroughly, then add to the sauce. Heat through gently. Season the vegetables to taste. Pour some sauce into small ramekins and garnish with 4 sprigs of thyme. Serve immediately with the roasted vegetables and the sauce to dip.

Roasted Butternut Squash

Serves 4

500 g/1 lb 1 oz butternut squash
4 garlic cloves, peeled and crushed
1 tbsp olive oil
salt and freshly ground black pepper
1 tbsp walnut oil, or use olive oil
4 medium-sized leeks, trimmed,
cleaned and thinly sliced
1 tbsp black mustard seeds
300 g can cannellini beans, drained
and rinsed
125 g/4 oz fine French beans, halved
150 ml/¹/₄ pint vegetable stock
50 g/2 oz rocket
2 tbsp freshly snipped chives
fresh chives, to garnish

To serve:
4 tbsp fromage frais
mixed salad

Fit the extender to the halogen oven bowl and place the low rack inside. Set the oven to 200°C/400°F. Cut the butternut squash in half lengthways and scoop out all of the seeds.

Score the squash in a diamond pattern with a sharp knife. Mix the garlic with the olive oil and brush over the cut surfaces of the squash, then add seasoning. Put on an ovenproof tray or use a roasting tin. Roast for 30– 40 minutes until tender. Reserve and keep warm.

Pour the walnut oil (or use olive oil) into an ovenproof dish and heat on the hob for 2 minutes. Add the leeks and mustard seeds. Stir and place in the oven. Cook for 10 minutes, then stir in the drained cannellini beans, French beans and vegetable stock. Close the lid and cook for 10–12 minutes until the French beans are tender.

Remove from the oven and stir in the rocket, chives and more seasoning. Stir the bean mixture into the cooked squash. Garnish with a few snipped chives and serve immediately with the fromage frais and a mixed salad.

Aubergine Ravioli Parmigiana

Serves 6

4 tbsp olive oil
1 large onion, peeled and finely chopped
2–3 garlic cloves, peeled and crushed
2 x 400 g cans chopped tomatoes
2 tsp brown sugar
1 dried bay leaf
1 tsp dried oregano
1 tsp dried basil
2 tbsp freshly shredded basil
salt and freshly ground black pepper
2–3 medium aubergines, sliced crossways 1 cm/$\frac{1}{2}$ inch thick
2 medium eggs, beaten with 1 tbsp water
125 g/4 oz dried breadcrumbs
75 g/3 oz freshly grated Parmesan cheese
400 g/14 oz mozzarella cheese, thinly sliced
250 g/9 oz cheese-filled ravioli, cooked and drained

Fit the extender to the halogen oven bowl and place the low rack inside. Set the oven to 180˚C/350˚F. Heat 2 tablespoons of the olive oil in a large, ovenproof dish. Add the onion and garlic and cook for 5 minutes, or until softened. Stir before adding the tomatoes, sugar, bay leaf, dried oregano and basil. Place in the oven and cook for 20–25 minutes until thickened and reduced. Remove from the oven and stir in the fresh basil and season to taste with salt and pepper. Remove the tomato sauce from the oven and reserve.

Meanwhile, heat the remaining olive oil in a large, heavy-based frying pan over a high heat. Dip the aubergine slices in the egg mixture, then in the breadcrumbs. Cook in batches until golden on both sides. Drain on absorbent kitchen paper. Add more oil between batches if necessary.

Spoon a little tomato sauce into the base of a lightly oiled baking dish that will fit in the oven. Cover with a layer of aubergine slices, a sprinkling of Parmesan cheese, a layer of mozzarella cheese, then more sauce. Repeat the layers, then cover the sauce with a layer of cooked ravioli. Continue to layer in this way, ending with a layer of mozzarella cheese. Sprinkle the top with Parmesan cheese.

Drizzle with a little extra olive oil if liked. Place on the rack in the oven and bake for 30 minutes, or until golden brown and bubbling. Serve immediately.

Baby Roast Potato Salad

Serves 4

350 g/12 oz small shallots
700 g/1¹/₂ lb small, even-sized
new potatoes
2 tbsp olive oil
sea salt and freshly ground
black pepper
2 medium courgettes
175 g/6 oz cherry tomatoes
2 fresh rosemary sprigs
150 ml/¹/₄ pint sour cream
2 tbsp freshly snipped chives

Place the low rack in the halogen oven and set the oven to 200°C/400°F. Trim the shallots but leave the skins on. Put in a saucepan of lightly salted, boiling water with the potatoes and cook for 8 minutes. Drain and separate the shallots and plunge them into cold water for 1 minute.

Pour the oil into a roasting tin or ovenproof dish that fits in the oven. Peel the shallots – the skins should now come away easily. Place in the roasting tin with the potatoes and toss in the oil to coat. Sprinkle with a little sea salt. Place on the rack and roast in the oven for 25–30 minutes.

Meanwhile, trim the courgettes, halve lengthways and cut into 5 cm/ 2 inch chunks. Remove the roasting tin from the oven and add the courgette chunks to the roasting tin, then stir well.

Pierce the tomato skins with a sharp knife. Add to the roasting tin together with the rosemary. Return to the oven and continue to roast for 10–15 minutes until all the vegetables are tender. Remove the rosemary and discard. Grind a little black pepper over the vegetables.

Spoon into a wide serving bowl. Mix together the sour cream and chives and drizzle over the vegetables just before serving.

Red Pepper Basil Tart

Serves 4–6

For the olive pastry:

225 g/8 oz plain flour
pinch salt
1 medium egg, lightly beaten, plus
1 egg yolk
3 tbsp olive oil
50 g/2 oz pitted black olives,
finely chopped

For the filling:

2 large red peppers, quartered
and deseeded
175 g/6 oz mascarpone cheese
4 tbsp milk
2 medium eggs
3 tbsp freshly chopped basil
salt and freshly ground
black pepper
fresh basil, sprig, to garnish
mixed salad, to serve

Place the high rack in the halogen oven and set the oven to 200˚C/ 400˚F. Sift the flour and salt into a bowl. Make a well in the centre. Stir together the egg, oil and 1 tablespoon tepid water. Add to the dry ingredients, drop in the olives and mix to a dough. Knead on a lightly floured surface for a few seconds until smooth, then wrap in clingfilm and chill in the refrigerator for 30 minutes. Roll out the pastry and use to line a 23 cm/9 inch, loose-bottomed, fluted flan tin. Cover and chill in the refrigerator for 20 minutes.

Place the peppers on the high rack in the oven and cook for 10 minutes, or until the skins are blackened and blistered. Remove from the oven and place them in a polythene bag, cool for 10 minutes, then remove the skin and slice. Replace the high rack with the low rack.

Line the pastry case with kitchen foil or baking parchment weighed down with baking beans, place on the low rack and bake in the oven for 10 minutes. Remove the kitchen foil and beans and bake for a further 5 minutes. Reduce the oven temperature to 180˚C/350˚F.

Beat the mascarpone cheese until smooth. Gradually add the milk and eggs. Stir in the peppers and basil and season to taste. Spoon into the flan case and bake for 25–30 minutes until lightly set. Garnish with a sprig of fresh basil and serve immediately with a mixed salad.

Tomato Courgette Herb Tart

Serves 4

4 tbsp olive oil
1 onion, peeled and
finely chopped
3 garlic cloves, peeled and crushed
350 g/12 oz prepared puff pastry,
thawed if frozen
1 small egg, beaten
2 tbsp freshly chopped rosemary
2 tbsp freshly chopped parsley
175 g/6 oz rindless fresh soft
goats' cheese
4 ripe plum tomatoes, sliced
1 medium courgette, trimmed
and sliced
thyme sprigs, to garnish

Place the low rack in the halogen oven and set the oven to 200°C/400°F. Pour 2 tablespoons of the oil into a saucepan and add the onion and garlic. Cook for 4–6 minutes until softened. Remove from the heat and reserve.

Roll out the pastry on a lightly floured surface, and cut out a 23 cm/ 9 inch circle.

Brush the pastry with a little beaten egg, then prick all over with a fork. Place on a dampened, ovenproof tray.

Mix together the onion, garlic and herbs with the goats' cheese and spread over the pastry. Arrange the tomatoes and courgettes over the goats' cheese and drizzle with the remaining oil.

Place on the low rack and bake for 20–25 minutes until the pastry is golden brown and risen with the topping bubbling. Garnish with the thyme sprigs and serve immediately.

Layered Cheese Herb Potato Cake

Serves 4

900 g/2 lb waxy potatoes
3 tbsp freshly snipped chives
2 tbsp freshly chopped parsley
225 g/8 oz mature Cheddar cheese
2 large egg yolks
1 tsp paprika
125 g/4 oz fresh white breadcrumbs
50 g/2 oz almonds, toasted and
roughly chopped
salt and freshly ground black pepper
50 g/2 oz butter, melted
mixed salad or steamed vegetables,
to serve

Place the low rack in the halogen oven and set the oven to 180˚C/350˚F. Lightly oil and line the base of a 20.5 cm/8 inch, round cake tin with lightly oiled baking parchment. Peel and thinly slice the potatoes and reserve. Stir the chives, parsley, cheese and egg yolks together in a small bowl and reserve. Mix the paprika into the breadcrumbs.

Sprinkle the almonds over the base of the lined tin. Cover with half the potatoes, arranging them in layers, then sprinkle with the paprika and breadcrumb mixture and season to taste with salt and pepper.

Spoon the cheese and herb mixture over the breadcrumbs with a little more seasoning, then arrange the remaining potatoes on top. Drizzle over the melted butter and press the surface down firmly.

Bake in the oven for 1–1¼ hours until golden and cooked through. (Cover the top with kitchen foil if browning too much). Remove from the oven and leave to rest for 10 minutes before carefully turning out and serving in thick wedges. Serve immediately with salad or freshly cooked vegetables.

Courgette Lasagne

Serves 8

2 tbsp olive oil
1 medium onion, peeled and
finely chopped
225 g/8 oz mushrooms, wiped and
thinly sliced
3–4 courgettes, trimmed and
thinly sliced
2 garlic cloves, peeled and
finely chopped
$^1/_2$ tsp dried thyme
1–2 tbsp freshly chopped basil or
flat-leaf parsley
salt and freshly ground
black pepper
1 quantity prepared white sauce
(see page 68)
350 g/12 oz precooked
lasagne sheets
225 g/8 oz mozzarella
cheese, grated
50 g/2 oz Parmesan cheese, grated
400 g can chopped
tomatoes, drained

Place the low rack in the halogen oven and set the oven to 200°C/400°F. Heat the oil in a large frying pan, add the onion and cook for 3–5 minutes. Add the mushrooms, cook for 2 minutes, then add the courgettes and cook for a further 3–4 minutes until tender. Stir in the garlic, thyme and basil or parsley and season to taste with salt and pepper. Remove from the heat and reserve.

Spoon one third of the white sauce onto the base of a lightly oiled, large baking dish. Arrange a layer of lasagne over the sauce. Spread half the courgette mixture over the pasta, then sprinkle with some of the mozzarella and some of the Parmesan cheese. Repeat with more white sauce and another layer of lasagne, and then cover with half the drained tomatoes.

Cover the tomatoes with lasagne, the remaining courgette mixture, and some mozzarella and Parmesan cheese. Repeat the layers, ending with a layer of lasagne sheets, white sauce and the remaining Parmesan cheese. Bake in the oven for 25–30 minutes until golden. Serve immediately.

Vegetable & Goats' Cheese Pizza

Serves 4

125 g/4 oz baking potato
1 tbsp olive oil
225 g/8 oz strong white flour
$^1/_2$ tsp salt
1 tsp easy-blend dried yeast

For the topping:

1 medium aubergine, thinly sliced
2 small courgettes, trimmed and
sliced lengthways
1 yellow pepper, quartered
and deseeded
1 red onion, peeled and sliced into
very thin wedges
5 tbsp olive oil
175 g/6 oz cooked new
potatoes, halved
400 g can chopped tomatoes,
drained
2 tsp freshly chopped oregano
125 g/4 oz mozzarella cheese,
cut into small cubes
125 g/4 oz goats' cheese, crumbled

Set the halogen oven to 220°C/425°F and put the high rack in the oven. Cook the potato in lightly salted, boiling water until tender. Peel and mash with the olive oil until smooth.

Sift the flour and salt into a bowl. Stir in the yeast. Add the mashed potato and 150 ml/$^1/_4$ pint warm water and mix to a soft dough. Knead for 5–6 minutes until smooth. Put the dough in a bowl, cover with clingfilm and leave to rise in a warm place for 30 minutes.

To make the topping, arrange the aubergine, courgettes, pepper and onion, skin-side up, on the high rack, lined with kitchen foil if liked, and brush with 4 tablespoons of the oil. Place in the oven and grill for 4 minutes. Turn the vegetables and brush with the remaining oil. Grill for a further 3–4 minutes until tender. Cool, skin and slice the pepper. Put all of the vegetables in a bowl, add the halved new potatoes and toss gently together. Reserve.

Briefly knead the dough, then roll out to a 23 cm/9 inch round. Mix the tomatoes and oregano together and spread over the pizza base. Scatter over the mozzarella cheese. Put the pizza on the high rack, lined with kitchen foil if liked, or use a large, ovenproof plate that fits in the oven. Bake for 8 minutes. Arrange the vegetables and goats' cheese on top and bake for 8–10 minutes. Serve.

Leek & Potato Tart

Serves 6

225 g/8 oz plain flour
pinch salt
150 g/5 oz butter, cubed
50 g/2 oz walnuts, very finely
chopped
1 large egg yolk

For the filling:

450 g/1 lb leeks, trimmed and
thinly sliced
40 g/1¹/₂ oz butter
450 g/1 lb large new potatoes,
scrubbed
300 ml/¹/₂ pint sour cream
3 medium eggs, lightly beaten
175 g/6 oz Gruyère cheese, grated
freshly grated nutmeg
salt and freshly ground black pepper
fresh chives, to garnish

Place the low rack in the halogen oven and set the oven to 190°C/375°F. Sift the flour and salt into a bowl. Rub in the butter until the mixture resembles breadcrumbs. Stir in the nuts. Mix together the egg yolk and 3 tablespoons cold water. Sprinkle over the dry ingredients. Mix to form a dough.

Knead on a lightly floured surface for a few seconds, then wrap in clingfilm and chill in the refrigerator for 20 minutes. Roll out and use to line a 20.5 cm/ 8 inch springform tin or very deep flan tin. Chill for a further 30 minutes.

Cook the leeks in the butter over a high heat for 2–3 minutes, stirring constantly. Lower the heat and cover with a lid or foil. Cook for 10–12 minutes, until soft, stirring occasionally. Remove the leeks from the heat.

Cook the potatoes in boiling salted water for 15 minutes, or until tender. Drain and thickly slice. Add to the leeks. Stir the sour cream into the leeks and potatoes, followed by the eggs, cheese, nutmeg and salt and pepper. Pour into the pastry case and level the top. Place in the oven and bake for 20 minutes.

Reduce the oven temperature to 180°C/350°F and cover the top with kitchen foil if browning too quickly. Cook for a further 20–25 minutes until the filling is set. Garnish with chives and serve immediately.

Cheese & Onion Oat Pie

Serves 4

1 tbsp sunflower oil, plus 1 tsp
25 g/1 oz butter
2 medium onions, peeled
and sliced
1 garlic clove, peeled and crushed
150 g/5 oz porridge oats
125 g/4 oz mature Cheddar
cheese, grated
2 medium eggs, lightly beaten
2 tbsp freshly chopped parsley
salt and freshly ground black
pepper
275 g/10 oz baking potatoes,
peeled

Place the low rack in the halogen oven and set the oven to 180°C/350°F. Heat the oil and half the butter in a saucepan and add the onions and garlic. Cook for 8–10 minutes until soft. Remove from the heat and reserve.

Spread the oats out on a baking tray or ovenproof plate and toast in the oven for 10 minutes. Stir occasionally. Leave to cool, then add to the onions with the cheese, eggs and parsley. Season to taste with salt and pepper and mix well.

Line the base of a 20.5 cm/8 inch, round sandwich tin with baking parchment and oil well. Thinly slice the potato and arrange the slices on the base, overlapping them slightly.

Spoon the cheese and oat mixture on top of the potato, spreading evenly with the back of a spoon. Cover with kitchen foil and bake for 30 minutes.

Invert the pie onto a baking tray or plate so that the potatoes are on top. Carefully remove the tin and lining paper.

Melt the remaining butter and carefully brush over the potato topping. Add the high rack to the oven and place the potato cake on top. Cook for 10–12 minutes until the potatoes are lightly browned. Cut into wedges and serve.

Potato & Goats' Cheese Tart

Serves 6

275 g/10 oz prepared shortcrust pastry, thawed if frozen

550 g/1 lb 3 oz small waxy potatoes

beaten egg, for brushing

2 tbsp sun-dried tomato paste

$^1/_4$ tsp chilli powder, or to taste

1 large egg

150 ml/$^1/_4$ pint sour cream

150 ml/$^1/_4$ pint milk

2 tbsp freshly snipped chives

salt and freshly ground black pepper

300 g/11 oz goats' cheese, sliced

salad and warm crusty bread, to serve

Place the high rack in the halogen oven and set the oven to 200˚C/400˚F. Roll the pastry out on a lightly floured surface and use to line a 23 cm/ 9 inch, fluted flan tin. Chill in the refrigerator for 30 minutes.

Scrub the potatoes, place in a large saucepan of lightly salted water and bring to the boil. Simmer for 15 minutes, or until the potatoes are tender. Drain and reserve until cool enough to handle.

Line the pastry case with kitchen foil and baking beans and bake blind in the oven for 12 minutes. Remove from the oven and discard the foil and beans. Brush the base with a little beaten egg, then return to the oven and cook for a further 5 minutes. Remove from the oven. Reduce the oven to 180˚C/350˚F and replace the high rack with the low rack.

Cut the potatoes into 1 cm/$^1/_2$ inch thick slices; reserve. Spread the sun-dried tomato paste over the base of the pastry case, sprinkle with the chilli powder, then arrange the potato slices on top in a decorative pattern.

Beat together the egg, sour cream, milk and chives, then season to taste with salt and pepper. Pour over the potatoes. Arrange the goats' cheese on top of the potatoes. Bake in the oven for 30 minutes, or until golden brown and set. Serve immediately with salad and warm bread.

Melanzane Parmigiana

Serves 4

900 g/2 lb aubergines
salt and freshly ground black pepper
5 tbsp olive oil
1 red onion, peeled and chopped
$^1/_2$ tsp mild paprika
150 ml/$^1/_4$ pint dry red wine
150 ml/$^1/_4$ pint vegetable stock
400 g can chopped tomatoes
1 tsp tomato purée
1 tbsp freshly chopped oregano
175 g/6 oz mozzarella cheese,
thinly sliced
40 g/1$^1/_2$ oz Parmesan cheese,
coarsely grated
fresh basil sprig, to garnish

Place the high rack in the halogen oven and set the oven to 200°C/400°F. Cut the aubergines lengthways into thin slices. Sprinkle with salt and leave to drain in a colander over a bowl for 15 minutes.

Rinse the aubergine slices thoroughly under cold water, pat dry on absorbent kitchen paper and brush the aubergines with 2 tablespoons of the oil. Place on the rack and cook in batches, for 3 minutes on each side, until golden. Drain well on absorbent kitchen paper.

Heat 1 tablespoon of the olive oil in a saucepan and add the onion. Cook for 10 minutes, or until softened. Stir in the paprika with the wine, stock, tomatoes and tomato purée. Pour into an ovenproof dish. Replace the high rack with the low rack. Reduce the oven to 160°C/325°F and cook the tomato sauce mixture for 15–20 minutes until fairly thick. Remove from the oven and stir in the oregano and season to taste with salt and pepper.

Pour half of the tomato sauce into the base of a large, ovenproof dish that will fit in the oven. Cover with half the aubergine slices, and then top with the mozzarella. Cover with the remaining aubergine slices and pour over the remaining tomato sauce. Sprinkle with the grated Parmesan cheese. Place the dish in the oven and cook for 30 minutes, or until the aubergines are tender and the sauce is bubbling. Garnish with a sprig of fresh basil and cool for a few minutes before serving.

Italian Baked Tomatoes

Serves 4

1 tsp olive oil
4 beef tomatoes
salt
50 g/2 oz fresh white breadcrumbs
1 tbsp freshly snipped chives
1 tbsp freshly chopped parsley
125 g/4 oz button mushrooms, finely chopped
salt and freshly ground black pepper
25 g/1 oz fresh Parmesan cheese, grated

For the salad:

1/2 curly endive lettuce
1/2 small piece radicchio
2 tbsp olive oil
1 tsp balsamic vinegar
salt and freshly ground black pepper

Place the low rack in the halogen oven and set the oven to 180°C/350°F. Lightly oil a baking tray with the teaspoon of oil. Slice the tops off the tomatoes and remove all the flesh, then sieve into a large bowl. Sprinkle a little salt inside the tomato shells, and then place them upside down on a plate while the filling is prepared.

Mix the sieved tomato with the breadcrumbs, fresh herbs and mushrooms and season with salt and pepper. Place the tomato shells on the prepared baking tray and fill with the tomato and mushroom mixture. Sprinkle the cheese on the top. Bake in the oven for 15–20 minutes until golden brown.

Meanwhile, prepare the salad. Arrange the endive and radicchio on individual serving plates and mix the remaining ingredients together in a small bowl to make the dressing. Season to taste.

When the tomatoes are cooked, allow to rest for 5 minutes, then place on the prepared plates and drizzle over a little dressing. Serve warm.

Baked Macaroni Cheese

Serves 8

450 g/1 lb macaroni
75 g/3 oz butter
1 onion, peeled and finely chopped
40 g/1^1/$_2$ oz plain flour
1 litre/1^3/$_4$ pints milk
1–2 dried bay leaves
^{1}/$_2$ tsp dried thyme
salt and freshly ground black pepper
cayenne pepper
freshly grated nutmeg
2 small leeks, trimmed, finely
chopped, cooked and drained
1 tbsp Dijon mustard
400 g/14 oz mature Cheddar
cheese, grated
2 tbsp dried breadcrumbs
2 tbsp freshly grated Parmesan
cheese
basil sprig, to garnish

Fit the extender to the halogen oven bowl and place the low rack in the oven. Set the oven to 190˚C/375˚F. Bring a large pan of lightly salted water to a rolling boil. Add the macaroni and cook according to the packet instructions, or *al dente*. Drain thoroughly and reserve.

Meanwhile, melt 50 g/2 oz of the butter in a large saucepan, add the onion and cook, stirring frequently, for 5–7 minutes until softened. Sprinkle in the flour and cook, stirring constantly, for 2 minutes. Remove the pan from the heat, stir in the milk, return to the heat and cook, stirring, until a smooth sauce has formed.

Add the bay leaf and thyme to the sauce and season to taste with salt, black and cayenne pepper and freshly grated nutmeg. Simmer for about 15 minutes, stirring frequently, until thickened and smooth.

Remove the sauce from the heat. Add the cooked leeks, mustard and Cheddar cheese and stir until the cheese has melted. Stir in the macaroni, then tip into a lightly oiled baking dish that fits in the oven.

Sprinkle the breadcrumbs and Parmesan cheese over the macaroni. Dot with the remaining butter. Place on the rack and bake in the oven for 30–35 minutes until golden. Garnish with a basil sprig and serve immediately.

Spinach Mascarpone Pizza

Serves 2–4

For the pizza dough:
225 g/8 oz strong plain flour
1/2 tsp salt
1/4 tsp quick-acting dried yeast
150 ml/1/4 pint warm water
1 tbsp extra virgin olive oil

For the topping:
3 tbsp olive oil
1 large red onion, peeled and chopped
2 garlic cloves, peeled and finely sliced
450 g/1 lb frozen spinach, thawed and drained
salt and freshly ground black pepper
3 tbsp passata
125 g/4 oz mascarpone cheese
1 tbsp toasted pine nuts

Place the high rack in the halogen oven and set the oven to 200˚C/400˚F. Sift the flour and salt into a bowl and stir in the yeast. Make a well in the centre and gradually add the water and oil to form a soft dough.

Knead the dough on a floured surface for about 5 minutes until smooth and elastic. Place in a lightly oiled bowl and cover with clingfilm. Leave to rise in a warm place for 1 hour.

Knock the pizza dough with your fist a few times, shape and roll out thinly on a lightly floured board, to form 25.5 cm/10 inch round. Place on a lightly floured baking tray and lift the edge to make a little rim.

Heat half the oil in a frying pan and gently fry the onion and garlic until soft and starting to change colour.

Squeeze out any excess water from the spinach and chop finely. Add to the onion and garlic with the remaining olive oil. Season to taste with salt and pepper.

Spread the passata on the pizza dough and top with the spinach mixture. Mix the mascarpone with the pine nuts and dot over the pizza. Place on the rack in the oven and bake for 12–15 minutes. Transfer to a large plate and serve immediately.

Vegetable Cassoulet

Serves 4

225 g/8 oz dried haricot beans,
soaked overnight
2 medium onions
1 bay leaf
550 g/1 lb 3 oz large potatoes,
peeled and cut into
1 cm/¹/₂ inch slices
5 tsp olive oil
1 large garlic clove, peeled
and crushed
2 leeks, trimmed and sliced
200 g can chopped tomatoes
1 tsp dark muscovado sugar
1 tbsp freshly chopped thyme
2 tbsp freshly chopped parsley
salt and freshly ground black pepper
3 courgettes, trimmed and sliced
50 g/2 oz fresh white breadcrumbs
25 g/1 oz Cheddar cheese,
finely grated

Fit the extender to the halogen oven bowl and place the low rack in the oven. Set the oven to 160˚C/325˚F. Drain the beans, rinse under cold running water and put in a saucepan. Pour in 1.4 litres/2¹/₂ pints cold water. Bring to a rapid boil and cook for 10 minutes, drain and place in an ovenproof dish with a lid. Peel one of the onions and add to the beans with the bay leaf. Cover with boiling water and add the lid. Place in the oven and cook for 50 minutes, or until the beans are almost tender. Drain the beans, reserving the liquor, but discarding the onion and bay leaf.

Meanwhile, cook the potatoes in a saucepan of lightly salted boiling water for 6–7 minutes until almost tender when tested with the point of a knife. Drain and reserve.

Peel and chop the remaining onion. Heat the oil in a frying pan and cook the onion with the garlic and leeks for 10 minutes until softened. Stir in the tomatoes, sugar, thyme and parsley. Stir in the beans with 300 ml/¹/₂ pint of the reserved liquor and season to taste. Simmer, uncovered, for 5 minutes.

Layer the potato slices, courgettes and ladlefuls of the bean mixture in a large, ovenproof casserole dish that fits in the oven. To make the topping, mix together the breadcrumbs and cheese and sprinkle over the top. Bake for 40 minutes, or until the vegetables are cooked through and the topping is golden brown and crisp. Serve immediately.

Puddings
AND Desserts

For those with a sweet tooth, no meal is complete without a dessert. For a bowlful of pure indulgence, just whip up the Chocolate Sponge Pudding or, if fruity is more your thing, give the Baked Stuffed Amaretti Peaches a go. Aside from puddings, halogen cooking is a great way to bake sweet treats for the cupboard or lunchboxes; why not delight with a batch of Choc Chip Cookies or Apple & Cinnamon Crumble Bars.

Golden Castle Pudding

Serves 4–6

125 g/4 oz butter
125 g/4 oz caster sugar
few drops vanilla extract
2 medium eggs, beaten
125 g/4 oz self-raising flour
4 tbsp golden syrup
crème fraîche or ready-made
custard, to serve

Fit the extender to the halogen oven bowl and place the high rack in the oven. Set the oven to 175°C/350°F. Lightly oil four to six individual pudding basins and place a small circle of baking parchment in the base of each one.

Place the butter and caster sugar in a large bowl, then beat together until the mixture is pale and creamy. Stir in the vanilla extract and gradually add the beaten eggs, a little at a time. Add a tablespoon of flour after each addition of egg and beat well.

When the mixture is smooth, add the remaining flour and fold in gently. Add a tablespoon of water and mix to form a soft mixture that will drop easily off a spoon.

Spoon the mixture into each basin, allowing enough space for the puddings to rise. Place on a baking sheet or straight onto the rack. Bake in the oven for about 15–16 minutes until firm and golden brown.

Allow the puddings to stand for 5 minutes, then turn out onto individual serving plates and discard the small parchment circles.

Warm the golden syrup in a small saucepan and pour a little over each pudding. Serve hot with the crème fraîche or custard.

Apple Cinnamon Crumble Bars

Makes 16

450 g/1 lb Bramley cooking
apples, peeled and
roughly chopped
50 g/2 oz raisins
50 g/2 oz caster sugar
1 tsp ground cinnamon
grated zest of 1 lemon
200 g/7 oz plain flour
250 g/9 oz soft light brown sugar
½ tsp bicarbonate of soda
150 g/5 oz rolled oats
150 g/5 oz butter, melted
crème fraîche or whipped cream,
to serve

Fit the extender to the halogen oven bowl and place the high rack in the oven. Set the oven to 180°C/350°F. Put the apples, raisins, sugar, cinnamon and lemon zest into a saucepan over a high heat.

Cover and cook for 15 minutes, stirring occasionally, until the apple is cooked through. Remove the cover, then stir well with a wooden spoon to break up the apple completely.

Cook for a further 5 minutes, or until thickened. Allow to cool. Lightly oil and line a 20.5 cm/8 inch, square cake tin with baking parchment.

Mix together the flour, sugar, bicarbonate of soda, rolled oats and butter until well mixed and crumbly. Spread half of the flour mixture into the bottom of the prepared tin and press down. Pour over the apple mixture.

Sprinkle over the remaining flour mixture and press down lightly. Bake in the oven for 20–25 minutes until golden brown. Cover the top with kitchen foil if browning too quickly and remember to scrunch the foil under the rim of the tin so it stays in place. Remove from the oven to cool before cutting into slices. Serve the bars warm or cold with crème fraîche or whipped cream.

Baked Stuffed Amaretti Peaches

Serves 4

4 ripe peaches
grated zest of 1 lemon
75 g/3 oz Amaretti biscuits
50 g/2 oz chopped blanched
almonds, toasted
50 g/2 oz pine nuts, toasted
40 g/1 1/2 oz light muscovado sugar
50 g/2 oz butter
1 medium egg yolk
2 tsp clear honey
crème fraîche or Greek yogurt,
to serve

Fit the extender to the halogen oven bowl and place the high rack in the oven. Set the oven to 180˚C/350˚F. Halve the peaches and remove the stones. Take a very thin slice from the bottom of each peach half so that it will sit flat and arrange in the dish.

Crush the Amaretti biscuits lightly and put into a large bowl. Add the almonds, pine nuts, sugar, lemon zest and butter. Working with the fingertips, mix together until the mixture resembles coarse breadcrumbs. Add the egg yolk and mix well until the mixture is just binding.

Divide the Amaretti and nut mixture between the peach halves, pressing down lightly. Bake in the oven for 15 minutes, or until the peaches are tender and the filling is golden. Remove from the oven and drizzle with the honey.

Place 2 peach halves on each serving plate and spoon over a little crème fraîche or Greek yogurt, then serve.

Lemon Butter Biscuits

Makes 14–18

175 g/6 oz butter, softened, plus
2 tsp for greasing
75 g/3 oz caster sugar
175 g/6 oz plain flour
75 g/3 oz cornflour
finely grated zest of 1 lemon
2 tbsp caster sugar, to decorate

Fit the extender to the halogen oven bowl and place the high rack in the oven. Set the oven to 180°C/350°F. Lightly grease or line with baking parchment two baking trays that will fit in the oven, or line the rack with kitchen foil. Place the butter and sugar into a bowl and beat together with the sugar until light and fluffy.

Sift in the flour and cornflour, add the lemon zest and mix together with a flat-bladed knife to form a soft dough.

Place the dough on a lightly floured surface, knead lightly and roll out thinly. Use biscuit cutters to cut out fancy shapes, re-rolling the trimmings to make more biscuits. Carefully lift each biscuit onto a baking tray with a palette knife, and then prick lightly with a fork.

Bake for 12–15 minutes until the biscuits are beginning to colour. Cool on the baking trays for 5 minutes, then place on a wire rack. Once completely cool, dust with caster sugar.

Chocolate Sponge Pudding

Serves 3–4

75 g/3 oz butter
75 g/3 oz caster sugar
50 g/2 oz plain dark chocolate, melted
50 g/2 oz self-raising flour
25 g/1 oz drinking chocolate
1 large egg
1 tbsp icing sugar, for dusingt
crème fraîche, to serve

For the fudge sauce:

50 g/2 oz soft light brown sugar
1 tbsp cocoa powder
40 g/1½ oz pecan nuts, roughly chopped
25 g/1 oz caster sugar
300 ml/½ pint hot, strong black coffee

Fit the extender to the halogen oven bowl and place the high rack in the oven. Set the oven to 170°C/325°F. Oil a 900 ml/1½ pint pie dish.

Cream the butter and the sugar together in a large bowl until light and fluffy. Stir in the melted chocolate, flour, drinking chocolate and egg and mix together. Turn the mixture into the prepared dish and level the surface.

To make the fudge sauce, blend the brown sugar, cocoa powder and pecan nuts together and sprinkle evenly over the top of the pudding. Stir the caster sugar into the hot black coffee until it has dissolved. Carefully pour the coffee over the top of the pudding.

Bake in the oven for 20– 25 minutes until the top is firm to the touch. Cover with kitchen foil if browning too much. Allow to stand for 5 minutes. There will now be a rich sauce underneath the sponge. Remove from the oven, dust with icing sugar and serve hot with crème fraîche.

Rich Double-crust Plum Pie

Serves 6

For the pastry:
75 g/3 oz butter
75 g/3 oz white vegetable fat
225 g/8 oz plain flour, plus extra
for dusting
2 medium egg yolks

For the filling:
450 g/1 lb fresh plums,
preferably Victoria
50 g/2 oz caster sugar, plus a little
extra for sprinkling
1 tbsp milk

Fit the extender to the halogen oven bowl and place the high rack in the oven. Set the oven to 180°C/350°F. Make the pastry by rubbing the butter and white vegetable fat into the flour until it resembles fine breadcrumbs, or blend in a food processor. Add the egg yolks and enough water to make a soft dough. Knead lightly, then wrap and leave in the refrigerator for about 30 minutes. Meanwhile, prepare the fruit. Rinse and dry the plums, then cut in half and remove the stones. Slice the plums into chunks and cook in a saucepan with 25 g/1 oz of the sugar and 2 tablespoons water for 5–7 minutes until slightly softened. Remove from the heat and add the remaining sugar to taste and allow to cool.

Roll out half the chilled pastry on a lightly floured surface and use to line the base and sides of a 1.1 litre/2 pint pie dish. Allow the pastry to hang over the edge of the dish. Spoon in the plums. Roll out the remaining pastry to use as the lid and brush the edge with a little water. Wrap the pastry around the rolling pin and place over the plums. Press the edges together to seal and mark a decorative edge around the rim of the pastry by pinching with the thumb and forefinger or using the back of a fork. Brush the lid with milk, and make a few slits in the top. Use any trimmings to decorate the top of the pie with pastry leaves. Place on a baking tray and bake in the oven for 25–30 minutes, until golden brown. Cover with kitchen foil if browning too quickly. Sprinkle with a little caster sugar and serve hot or cold.

Traditional Oven Scones

Makes 6–8

225 g/8 oz self-raising flour
1 tsp baking powder
pinch salt
40 g/1 1/2 oz butter, cubed
15 g/1/2 oz caster sugar
150 ml/1/4 pint milk, plus
1 tbsp for brushing
1 tbsp plain flour, for dusting

Lemon & sultana scone variation:

50 g/2 oz sultanas
finely grated zest of 1/2 lemon
beaten egg, to glaze

Fit the extender to the halogen oven bowl and place the high rack in the oven. Set the oven to 180°C/350°F. Sift the flour, baking powder and salt into a large bowl. Rub in the butter until the mixture resembles fine breadcrumbs. Stir in the sugar and mix with enough milk to give a fairly soft dough.

Knead the dough on a lightly floured surface for a few seconds until smooth. Roll out until 2.5 cm/1 inch thick and stamp out six rounds with a floured plain cutter.

Place on an oiled baking tray and brush the tops with milk (do not brush it over the sides or the scones will not rise properly). Dust with a little plain flour.

Bake in the oven for 10–12 minutes until well risen and golden brown. Transfer to a wire rack and serve warm, or leave to cool completely. The scones are best eaten on the day of baking, but may be kept in an airtight container for up to 2 days.

For lemon and sultana scones, stir in the sultanas and lemon zest with the sugar. Roll out until 2 cm/3/4 inch thick and cut into 8 fingers, 10 x 2.5 cm/4 x 1 inch in size. Bake the scones as before, and glaze with beaten egg.

Chocolate Fruit Crumble

Serves 4

For the crumble:
125 g/4 oz plain flour
125 g/4 oz butter
75 g/3 oz soft light brown sugar
50 g/2 oz rolled porridge oats
50 g/2 oz hazelnuts, chopped

For the filling:
450 g/1 lb Bramley apples
1 tbsp lemon juice
50 g/2 oz sultanas
50 g/2 oz seedless raisins
50 g/2 oz soft light brown sugar
350 g/12 oz pears, peeled, cored and chopped
1 tsp ground cinnamon
125 g/4 oz plain dark chocolate, very roughly chopped
2 tsp caster sugar, for sprinkling

Place the low rack in the halogen oven and set the oven to 175°C/350°F. Lightly oil an ovenproof dish.

For the crumble, sift the flour into a large bowl. Cut the butter into small dice and add to the flour. Rub the butter into the flour until the mixture resembles fine breadcrumbs.

Stir the sugar, porridge oats and the chopped hazelnuts into the mixture and reserve.

For the filling, peel the apples, core and slice thickly. Place in a large, heavy-based saucepan with the lemon juice and 3 tablespoons water. Add the sultanas, raisins and the soft brown sugar. Bring slowly to the boil, cover and simmer over a gentle heat for 8–10 minutes, stirring occasionally, until the apples are slightly softened.

Remove the saucepan from the heat and leave to cool slightly before stirring in the pears, ground cinnamon and the chopped chocolate.

Spoon into the prepared ovenproof dish. Sprinkle the crumble evenly over the top, then bake in the oven for 25–30 minutes until the top is golden. Remove from the oven, sprinkle with the caster sugar and serve immediately.

Lemon Ginger Buns

Makes 15

175 g/6 oz butter or margarine
350 g/12 oz plain flour
2 tsp baking powder
1/2 tsp ground ginger
pinch salt
finely grated zest and juice of
1 lemon
175 g/6 oz soft light brown sugar
125 g/4 oz sultanas
75 g/3 oz chopped mixed peel
25 g/1 oz stem ginger,
finely chopped
1 medium egg

Place the low rack in the halogen oven and set the oven to 180°C/350°F. Cut the butter or margarine into small pieces and place in a large bowl.

Sift the flour, baking powder, ginger and salt together and add to the butter with the lemon zest. Using the fingertips, rub the butter into the flour and spice mixture until it resembles coarse breadcrumbs.

Stir in the sugar, sultanas, chopped mixed peel and stem ginger.

Add the egg and lemon juice to the mixture, then, using a round-bladed knife, stir together.

Place heaped tablespoons of the mixture onto lightly oiled baking trays or ovenproof plates, making sure that the spoonfuls of mixture are spaced well apart.

Using a fork, rough up the edges of the buns and bake in the oven for 12–15 minutes.

Leave the buns to cool for 5 minutes before transferring to a wire rack until cold, then serve. Otherwise, store the buns in an airtight container and eat within 3–5 days.

Poached Pears with Chocolate Sauce

Serves 4

2 small cinnamon sticks
125 g/4 oz caster sugar
300 ml/^{1}/$_2$ pint red wine
150 ml/^{1}/$_4$ pint water
thinly pared zest and juice of
1 small orange
4 firm pears
orange slices, to decorate
frozen vanilla yogurt, or ice cream,
to serve

Place the low rack in the halogen oven and set the oven to 170°C/325°F. Place the cinnamon sticks on the work surface and, with a rolling pin, slowly roll down the side of the cinnamon sticks to bruise. Place in a large, heavy-based saucepan.

Add the sugar, wine, water, pared orange zest and juice to the pan and bring slowly to the boil, stirring occasionally, until the sugar is dissolved. Pour into an ovenproof dish.

Meanwhile, peel the pears, leaving the stalks on.

Cut a thin slice from the base of each pear so that they stand upright, both for the cooking and to ensure they stand in the serving dish.

Stand the pears in the syrup; cover the pan, then place in the oven and cook for 20–30 minutes until tender.

Remove the pan from the heat and leave the pears to cool in the syrup, turning occasionally.

Arrange the pears on serving plates and spoon over the syrup. Decorate with the orange slices and serve with the yogurt or ice cream and any remaining juices.

Chocolate Chip Cookies

Makes 36

175 g/6 oz plain flour
pinch salt
1 tsp baking powder
$1/4$ tsp bicarbonate of soda
75 g/3 oz butter or margarine
50 g/2 oz soft light brown sugar
3 tbsp golden syrup
125 g/4 oz chocolate chips

Place the low rack in the halogen oven and set the oven to 170°C/325°F. Lightly oil three or four baking trays or ovenproof plates.

Sift the flour, salt, baking powder and bicarbonate of soda into a large bowl.

Cut the butter or margarine into small pieces and add to the flour mixture. Using two knives or the fingertips, rub in the butter or margarine until the mixture resembles coarse breadcrumbs.

Add the light brown sugar, golden syrup and chocolate chips. Mix together until a smooth dough forms.

Shape the mixture into small balls and arrange on the baking trays or plates, leaving enough space to allow them to expand. (These cookies do not increase in size by a great deal, but you need to allow a little space for expansion.)

Flatten the mixture slightly with the fingertips or the heel of the hand. Bake in the oven for 12–15 minutes until golden and cooked through.

Allow to cool slightly, then transfer the biscuits onto a wire rack to cool completely. Serve when cold or store in an airtight container.

Crunchy Rhubarb Crumble

Serves 6

125 g/4 oz plain flour
50 g/2 oz butter, softened
50 g/2 oz rolled oats
50 g/2 oz demerara sugar
1 tbsp sesame seeds
1/2 tsp ground cinnamon
450 g/1 lb fresh rhubarb
50 g/2 oz caster sugar
custard or cream, to serve

Fit the extender to the halogen oven bowl and place the high rack in the oven. Set the oven to 180°C/350°F. Place the flour in a large bowl and cut the butter into cubes. Add to the flour and rub in with the fingertips until the mixture resembles fine breadcrumbs, or blend for a few seconds in a food processor.

Stir in the rolled oats, demerara sugar, sesame seeds and cinnamon. Mix well and reserve.

Prepare the rhubarb by removing the thick ends of the stalks and cut diagonally into 2.5 cm/1 inch chunks. Wash thoroughly and pat dry with a clean tea towel. Place the rhubarb in a 1.1 litre/2 pint pie dish.

Sprinkle the caster sugar over the rhubarb and place in the oven for 10 minutes, or until the rhubarb is softened. Spoon the crumble mixture on top. Level the top of the crumble so that all the fruit is well covered and press down firmly. If liked, sprinkle the top with a little extra caster sugar.

Place on a baking tray and bake in the oven for 25–30 minutes until the fruit is soft and the topping is golden brown. Sprinkle the pudding with some more caster sugar and serve hot with custard or cream.

Rice Pudding

Serves 4

65 g/2¹/₂ oz pudding rice
50 g/2 oz granulated sugar
410 g can light evaporated milk
300 ml/¹/₂ pint semi-skimmed milk
pinch freshly grated nutmeg
25 g/1 oz butter
jam, to decorate

Place the low rack in the halogen oven and set the oven to 150˚C/300˚F. Lightly oil a 1.1 litre/2 pint ovenproof dish. Sprinkle the rice and the sugar into the dish and mix.

Bring the evaporated milk and milk to the boil in a small pan, stirring occasionally. Stir the milks into the rice and mix well until the rice is coated thoroughly. Sprinkle over the nutmeg, cover with kitchen foil and bake in the oven for 30 minutes.

Remove the pudding from the oven and stir well, breaking up any lumps. Cover with the same kitchen foil. Bake in the oven for a further 15 minutes. Remove from the oven and stir well again.

Dot the pudding with butter and bake for a further 45–60 minutes until the rice is tender and the skin is browned. Divide the pudding between four individual serving bowls. Top with a large spoonful of the jam and serve immediately.

Rhubarb Raspberry Cobbler

Serves 4

450 g/1 lb rhubarb, cut into chunks
175 g/6 oz raspberries
50 g/2 oz golden caster sugar
zest and juice of 1 orange

For the topping:

225 g/8 oz plain flour
2 tsp baking powder
50 g/2 oz butter, diced
50 g/2 oz caster sugar
150 ml/¼ pint milk
custard or single cream, to serve

Fit the extender to the halogen oven bowl and place the high rack in the oven. Set the oven to 180°C/350°F. Butter a 1.1 litre/2 pint ovenproof dish.

Mix the rhubarb chunks with the raspberries and sugar and place in the buttered dish. Finely grate the zest from the orange and reserve. Squeeze out the juice and add to the dish with the rhubarb. Cover the dish with a piece of kitchen foil and cook in the oven for 10–15 minutes until the fruit is softened. Remove from the oven and discard the kitchen foil.

For the topping, sift the flour and baking powder into a bowl and stir in the grated orange zest. Rub in the butter with your fingertips until the mixture resembles fine crumbs. Stir in the caster sugar and quickly add the milk. Mix with a fork to make a soft dough. (The mixture has to be made quickly, as the raising agent – baking powder – starts to activate as soon as liquid is added.)

Break off small pieces of the dough and roll into small balls and drop them on top of the fruit filling. Bake for about 20–25 minutes until the topping is firm and golden. Serve immediately with custard or single cream.

Eve's Pudding

Serves 4-6

450 g/1 lb cooking apples
175 g/6 oz blackberries
75 g/3 oz demerara sugar
grated zest of 1 lemon
125 g/4 oz caster sugar
125 g/4 oz butter
few drops vanilla extract
2 medium eggs, beaten
125 g/4 oz self-raising flour
1 tbsp icing sugar
ready-made custard, to serve

Fit the extender to the halogen oven bowl and place the low rack in the oven. Set the oven to 175°C/350°F. Butter a 1.1 litre/2 pint baking dish.

Peel, core and slice the apples and place a layer in the base of the dish. Sprinkle over some of the blackberries, a little demerara sugar and lemon zest. Continue to layer the apples and blackberries in this way until all the ingredients have been used. Cover with kitchen foil and cook in the oven for 10–15 minutes until the fruit has started to soften.

Cream the caster sugar and butter together until light and fluffy. Beat in the vanilla extract, and then the eggs a little at a time, adding a spoonful of flour after each addition. Fold in the remaining flour with a metal spoon or rubber spatula and mix well.

Spread the sponge mixture over the top of the fruit and level with the back of a spoon. Place the dish on a baking tray and bake in the oven for 25–30 minutes until the top is firm and golden brown. To test if the pudding is cooked, press the cooked sponge lightly with a clean finger – if it springs back, the sponge is cooked. Cover with kitchen foil if browning too quickly.

Dust the pudding with a little icing sugar and serve immediately with the custard.

Index